# Living IN THE Light
# Workbook

## A GUIDE FOR PERSONAL AND PLANETARY TRANSFORMATION

## SHAKTI GAWAIN

### WITH LAUREL KING

NATARAJ

Nataraj Publishing

*a division of*

New World Library
Novato, California

Nataraj Publishing

*a division of*

New World Library
Novato, California

Revised Edition © 1998 Shakti Gawain and Laurel King
Original Edition © 1991 Shakti Gawain and Laurel King

Cover Art: Nicholas Wilton
Back Cover Photograph: Max O'Neill
Text Design: Riba Taylor

ISBN: 1-57731-047-0

First Printing, November 1998

Printed in Canada

Distributed by Publishers Group West

10  9  8  7  6  5  4  3  2  1

# Acknowledgments

I'd like to acknowledge Laurel King, who created the first draft of this manuscript and a majority of the exercises.

I'd like to thank Leslie Keenan, the editor of the first edition, as well as Becky Benenate and Katherine Dieter, the editors of the revised edition.

Thanks to Kathy Altman for contributing some exercises and good ideas.

And thanks to Marc Allen without whom (as usual) this book would not have happened. . . .

# Table of Contents

# Introduction

In my book *Living in the Light: A Guide to Personal and Planetary Transformation*, I describe a challenge that I believe we human beings are facing at this point in the evolution of consciousness here on earth. The challenge is for each of us as individuals to reconnect with our deepest spiritual source and learn to live moment to moment, day by day, in accordance with the guidance of our own inner sense of truth. In order to do this, we must develop the ability to listen and follow our intuition — that deep inner guidance that we all have but most of us have learned to ignore.

With a little support and practice, most people can begin to connect with and trust their intuitive sense. As we learn to follow our inner guidance, it can lead us step by step in very practical ways to solve problems, dissolve limitation, and expand creativity in every area of our lives — health and well-being, relationships, career and finances, emotional healing, and spiritual development. The more we are able to trust ourselves and follow our inner truth, the richer and more fulfilled our lives become. And I believe that it is only through this type of individual personal commitment to a life of integrity and balance that we can heal and transform our world.

This workbook has been designed as an accompaniment or follow-up to *Living in the Light*. The order in which some sections appear has been modified to make this a more useable workbook. A few of the meditations and exercises from *Living in the Light* have been included in this book, but for the most part, they are new and different. The purpose of this workbook is to assist you in exploring more fully, deeply, and specifically how these ideas and principles can be applied usefully in your own life.

I recommend that, if possible, you read *Living in the Light* and do the meditations and exercises in that book before beginning this workbook. In some cases, however, that may not be necessary; you may find the workbook useful and valuable on its own. Trust your intuition about this!

I sincerely hope that this workbook will be a useful tool for you, and that you find it creative and fun as well.

With Love,
Shakti

# How to Use the Workbook

Each chapter of the workbook starts with a few introductory paragraphs followed by an exercise or a series of exercises. Some exercises are meditations; many of them involve writing or, occasionally, drawing. There is room to write and draw in the workbook itself (there's even extra space in the margins for notes). You may find, however, that you desire or require more room than given. If so, I suggest that you get a separate notebook and use all the space you need. You might want to use it as a journal of the process you go through while you are working on this material, recording your dreams, daily thoughts, feelings, and insights. You might also like to keep the workbook and refer back to it later, or go back and re-do certain exercises at another time. The book has been designed with plenty of space so that you can use it more than once.

I also suggest that you equip yourself with wonderful colored pens, pencils, and/or crayons and experiment with different ways of using them with this material. Go ahead and play with your creativity! After all, no one else ever needs to see what you do, unless you choose to show someone.

Since the workbook starts with the basic principles and builds on that foundation, you may wish to do most of the exercises in the order given. But if you desire, you can work only on the sections that attract you, or you can skip around. Some of you may take a few weeks to work through this material; others may experience a process that could extend over a few years! Trust your own process and do what feels right for you.

Some of you may find it beneficial to form a support group with a few friends and meet weekly or monthly, doing the exercises together and sharing your feelings and responses to the changes, challenges, and miracles you will be experiencing in your lives.

One very important note: The material in this workbook touches some very profound areas in the psyche and may bring up lots of emotions and feelings. It can be very important and helpful to have professional support from a good therapist in working through these feelings and issues — either in individual counseling or in a group setting. I am a great believer in therapy. I feel that most people on a path of consciousness need the insight offered by a professional therapist at certain times. Be sure to find one who feels truly supportive and trustworthy. Don't be afraid to interview several until you find someone with whom you feel comfortable. If you feel you can't afford professional therapy, alternatives for emotional support could include twelve-step programs such as Alcoholics Anonymous, Overeaters Anonymous, Al-Anon, Codependents Anonymous, Debtors Anonymous, and so on. The meetings are free and are available in most cities.

I wish you increasing energy, awareness, joy, creativity, prosperity, and aliveness as you continue your journey of discovery.

Love and Light,
Shakti

# The Foundation

The basic principles described in *Living in the Light*, which we will be exploring here, are these:

- You have a higher power within you.
- You can learn to listen to your higher power through your intuitive guidance.
- You are a spiritual being contained in physical form.
- You are a channel for the creative energy of the universe to come into the physical world.

By learning to follow your own intuitive guidance, you can bring your physical life increasingly into alignment with your spiritual being. As you bring your individual life into balance and integration you contribute greatly to the transformation of the world.

The exercises that follow will help define and clarify what these words mean to you. Each individual is unique. Therefore, each of you will experience your higher power, intuition, channeling, spirit and form in your own way. If your experiences differ from those of others, this is not an invalidation of the experience, but rather a celebration of your unique being. I hope you will enjoy your journey of discovery as you build your own foundation.

# The Higher Power Within You

The foundation for life in the new world is built on the understanding that there is a higher intelligence, a fundamental creative power or energy in the universe that is the source and substance of all existence. These words and concepts that have been used to describe this power are innumerable. Here are just a few:

| | | |
|---|---|---|
| God | Spirit | Inner Guidance |
| Goddess | Essence | Higher Self |
| Higher Power | Being | The Universe |
| Source | Soul | Life Force |
| The Tao | The Force | Cosmic Intelligence |
| Buddha Nature | The Light | Christ Consciousness |
| Great Spirit | I Am | All That Is |

This workbook begins with discovering your relationship with this higher power. Do you believe in this intelligence, or are you unsure of its existence? If you believe in it, are you willing to trust this power? If you are uncertain, are you willing to take a leap of faith and simply act as if you believe in it for a period of time to see what you experience?

Once we acknowledge this power within us and learn to trust it, we can open up to receiving guidance in our lives. Though this guidance may come in many forms, some unexpected or even unusual, it will eventually lead to increased joy, health, energy, and prosperity.

As we learn to trust in the higher power of the universe absolutely, we will begin to live in accordance with universal principles. We can then enjoy the more abundant, creative, healthy, and fulfilling lives that await us.

## EXERCISE 1

To trust a higher power completely, it is essential to have a concept of the higher power as trustworthy. Since we are human, we tend to attribute human qualities to that higher power, and sometimes the qualities we attribute are *not* ones that build trust.

People's concepts of God usually stem from the past. They are based on early religious training and/or family experiences. For many people, a higher power means an authority figure or parent that guided them as children. So, if the adults around them were powerful and loving or critical and punishing, those were the qualities they would attribute to God. For others, God is something they read about and learned about in church or from those around them. For many, it is a combination of concepts they've picked up from others, not an experience they've felt within themselves.

With this in mind, the following questions can help clarify and expand your vision of this intelligence and your relationship to it. In answering these questions, write down the first things that come to your mind. If you find yourself struggling, let go of the question and move on to the next.

A.  In the space below (and on the following page) list ten qualities of the God you learned about as a child. For example:

*1. frightening*       *3. powerful*
*2. big*               *4. judgmental*

1.                     4.




2.                     5.




3.                     6.

7.                          9.



8.                          10.

Are these qualities trustworthy?

B.  If your belief in a higher intelligence has changed since childhood and you now see or feel it differently, list ten qualities that you now attribute to this force. **For example:**

*1. energy source*
*2. loving*
*3. omnipotent*

1.                          6.



2.                          7.



3.                          8.



4.                          9.



5.                          10.

C. If you were to expand your belief in a higher power even further so that you totally trusted it at all times, what qualities would that power have?

**For example:**
1. *totally reliable*
2. *all-knowing*
3. *offers total acceptance*

1.                                    6.

2.                                    7.

3.                                    8.

4.                                    9.

5.                                    10.

D. Close your eyes. As you inhale, imagine you are breathing into your body all the positive qualities of that power; as you exhale, let go of and release any qualities unlike that power. For example, feel yourself breathing in light, knowledge, acceptance, love, strength, and energy; as you exhale, breathe out tiredness, tension, self-hatred, worry, etc.

## EXERCISE 2

To describe your higher power further, and to better understand your relationship with it, explore the following questions.

A.  Describe briefly what this power looks or feels like. Does it have a human, animal, or light form, or is it a presence or energy? Is it masculine or feminine in nature, or a combination of the two, or neither?

B.  What is your relationship with this power? Can you describe how and when you make contact with it? Do you contact this power in a particular physical location (church, temple, or other sacred place), through contact with nature, through meditation or prayer, dance, exercise, etc.? Do you feel this contact in your body, mind, emotions, or spirit, or a combination of two or more of these levels?

C.  If your relationship to your higher power were to grow and expand, how would you like it to be? For example, would you like to be in more consistent contact or would you like more specific guidance? Let yourself explore this ideal relationship.

D.  Close you eyes and spend a few minutes visualizing that power, presence, or being now. Imagine yourself having the kind of relationship you've always wanted with this force — feel, see, and experience it as real right now.

# Intuition

Our higher power speaks to us through our intuition. Your intuition is the "gut" feeling within you — the source of your deepest personal truth. If you are willing to listen carefully to this feeling, it will guide you through each step of your life journey. The wisdom of the universe is completely available to us. We only need to learn to listen within to attain it.

How do we get in touch with our intuition? There is no single answer to that question. The process is different for everyone. Some people listen for their intuitive guidance through formal meditation, others through their art, dance, sports, music, writing, walks through nature, or moments of stillness. Your intuition may actually come to you as an inner voice, or you may be guided by a strong feeling or hunch, an image, or an inner energy or vibration.

The following exercises will guide you in contacting your intuition and help you to recognize it clearly. The exercises also may help you realize that you're already in contact with your intuition.

## EXERCISE 3

### *Meditation*

Sit or lie down in a comfortable position in a quiet place. Close your eyes and relax. Take several slow, deep breaths, relaxing your body more with each breath. Relax your mind and let your thoughts drift, but don't hold onto any thought. Imagine that your mind becomes as quiet as a peaceful lake.

Now, focus your conscious awareness into a deep place in your body, in the area of your stomach or solar plexus. It should be the place in your body where you feel that your "gut feelings" reside. This is the physical place where you can most easily contact your intuition.

Imagine that you have a wise being living inside there. You might have an image of what this wise being looks like, or you might just sense that it is there. This wise being is really a part of you — your intuitive self. You can communicate with it by talking to it silently, making requests, or asking questions. Then relax, don't think too hard, and be open to receiving the answers. The answers may come in words or in feelings or images. The answers are usually very simple, they relate to the present moment (not the past or future), and they "feel right." If you don't receive an immediate answer, let go and go about your life. The answer will come later, either from inside of you in the form of a feeling or idea, or from outside through a person, a book, an event, or whatever.

For example, you might say, "Intuition, tell me what I need to know here. What do I need to do in this situation?"

Trust the feeling that you get and act on it. If it is truly your intuition, you will find that it leads to a feeling of greater aliveness and power, and more opportunities begin to open up for you. If it doesn't seem right, you may not have been truly acting from your intuition but from a different voice in you. Go back and ask for clarification.

It takes practice to hear and trust your intuition. The more you do it, the easier it will become. Eventually, you will be able to contact your intuition, ask yourself questions, and know that in that "wise being" within you, an incredible source of power and strength is available to answer your questions and guide you. As you grow more sensitive to this guidance from the intuitive feelings within, you will gain a sense of knowing what you need to do in any situation. Your intuitive power is always available to guide you whenever you need it. It will open to you as soon as you are willing to trust yourself and your inner knowledge.

## EXERCISE 4

Another good way to practice getting in touch with your intuition is through writing with your nondominant hand.

If you are right-handed, let your right hand represent your conscious, rational mind, and your left hand represent your intuitive mind. (If you're left-handed, reverse it). Use a different colored pen for each hand.

Write a simple question that is of importance to you with your dominant hand. Then, without thinking too much, begin to answer it with your other hand. This may feel difficult. (You'll feel like you're in kindergarten again!) Do it anyway. Continue the dialogue as long as it feels appropriate. You may be surprised at what you learn.

### Example:

Right hand: What direction should I go in my life now?
*Left hand: Don't worry where to go. Be here.*
Right hand: But what about my career?
*Left hand: Relax. Don't think so much. It will work out fine.*
       *Stop trying so hard.*

Contacting, listening to, and acting on our intuition is not always easy. This is where we can find ourselves in opposition to life as most of us have been taught to live it in the old world. In modern western civilization, we have learned to respect and even worship the rational, logical aspect of our being, and to dismiss, depreciate, or deny our intuition.

Once we accept the reality of a higher power that is channeled to us through our intuition, it becomes clear that many of our personal problems and the ills of the world are actually caused by our *not* following our intuition.

## EXERCISE 5

A. Go back in your mind and remember all the times you have acted against yourself — when you have not heeded the guidance of your intuition. List as many of these instances as you can in the space below. What were the results?

Examples:

1. *My intuition kept telling me to quit my job and I wouldn't listen.*
   Result: *My car broke down three times in one month on the way to work.*

2. *My intuition told me to slow down and stop working so hard but fear of financial insecurity caused me to keep pushing myself.*
   Result: *I ended up spraining my back and couldn't get out of bed for two weeks.*

3. *I felt I should approach my boss with doubts I had concerning risks the company was taking, but I didn't act on this.*
   Result: *The company went ahead with its plans and lost a large sum of money.*

1.

2.

3.

4.

5.

6.

7.

8.

9.

10.

B. Now recall all the times you have followed your intuition. List as many of them as possible in the space below, and write how it felt. What were the results?

1. *My intuition told me to sign up for an interior design class.*
   **Result:** *I love it and am now working part-time at a design center.*

2. *I felt my husband and I might have to separate unless we learned to communicate more openly, so we started seeing a counselor.*
   **Result:** *My husband and I are beginning to open up in new ways. We are less dependent on each other and are building a new relationship based on trust and communication.*

3. *I had a strong impulse to approach my boss with a creative idea.*
   **Result:** *He was impressed and encouraged me to explore it further.*

1.

2.

3.

4.

5.

6.

7.

8.

9.

10.

C.   Make a list of things you would do today if you totally trusted your intuition. What is your "gut feeling" telling you to do? Learning to trust your intuition is learning to stay in the moment. What would you do right now?

**Examples:**

1. *Relax more and stop trying so hard.*
2. *Call the friend I haven't seen in ages and see how he is.*
3. *Take a walk this afternoon.*
4. *Spend the evening at home instead of going out.*
5. *Sign up for that class I've been curious about.*

1.

2.

3.

4.

5.



6.



7.



8.



9.



10.

# Becoming a Creative Channel

To whatever degree you listen to and follow your intuition, you become a "creative channel" for the higher power of the universe. When you willingly follow where your creative energy leads, the higher power can come through you to manifest its creative work. When this happens, you will find yourself flowing with the energy, doing what you really want to do, and feeling the power of the universe moving through you to create or transform everything around you.

In using the word channel, I am *not* referring to the psychic process of trance channeling. Trance channeling involves a medium who goes into a trance state and allows another being to speak through him or her. By channeling, I mean being in touch with and bringing through the wisdom and creativity of *your own* deepest source. Being a channel is being fully and freely yourself and consciously knowing that you are a vehicle for the creativity of the universe.

Every creative genius has been a channel. Every masterwork has been created through the channeling process. Great works are not created by the personality alone. They arise from a deep inspiration on the universal level, and are then expressed and brought into form *through* the individual personality.

All of us are geniuses — each in our own unique way. But the nature of our individual genius is often hidden from us, buried under our efforts to conform to a reality that does not suit us. As long as we accept others' ideas of how we should live our lives, we will fail to hear the voice of our higher power, and our genius will remain an untapped potential within us. It is only when we listen to our intuitive voice and trust its guidance that we can learn to be ourselves and to allow our natural channel to open.

## EXERCISE 6

*Meditation*

To become a creative channel, you must risk being who you really are. This may feel like a risk because your true nature may not fit any prior pictures or images you had of yourself. This exercise can help you relax your expectations and allow you a glimpse of your true inner being.

Close your eyes and take a few deep breaths. Ask your intuition to show you an image of your essential self. Accept any image that comes forward. The image may come in a human form or it may be a color, an object, or animal. Regardless of the form, there is a message in whatever picture you receive. If the significance of the image is not obvious, ask for clarification of the message. Be patient. The message may be immediately clear, or it may be revealed at some later time. If you repeat this exercise at later times you may get different images, and each one will show you some aspect of yourself.

Describe your image in the space below and on the following page, either in words or in pictures.

## EXERCISE 7

To become a creative channel, you must risk doing what you really want.

In column 1, list all the things you really love to do that you are currently doing.

In column 2, list things you consistently do even though you don't want to do them.

| Column 1 | Column 2 | Column 3 |
|---|---|---|
| *Things I love that I do* | *Things I don't want to do* | *Things I love that I don't do* |

In column 3, list everything that you want to do but are not doing.

**Examples:**

| | | |
|---|---|---|
| 1. *Bicycling* | *Housecleaning* | *Traveling* |
| 2. *Spending time with friends* | *Making business calls* | *Gardening* |
| 3. *Dancing* | *Listening to my sister's concepts about her life* | *Playing the piano* |
| 4. *Cooking* | *Driving the kids to school* | *Working with people more* |

1.


2.


3.

4.

5.

6.

7.

8.

9.

10.

After completing your lists, think creatively about the things you don't enjoy: Are there other ways they could be handled? For example, could you delegate more to other people, hire someone to assist you, or trade with someone who is willing to do an exchange for something you can do? You might also try to organize the unpleasant things differently so that they're easier to do, or spend one hour a day or one day a week doing what you least enjoy and then reward yourself with something you enjoy most. Are there some things you could just stop doing? By reviewing the list creatively, you can consider new options without immediately assuming that change is impossible.

Now apply this process to the other two lists: Can you start doing more of what you love, especially the things you aren't now doing? Start with small steps — take a few minutes a day, or an hour a week, for something you want to do, or enroll in a class, or put aside a weekend for something special and different. Write down some ideas and make some specific plans in the space below and the following page.

## EXERCISE 8

*Meditation*

Sit or lie down in a comfortable position. Close your eyes. Take a deep breath and relax your body. Take another deep breath and relax your mind. Continue to breathe slowly and deeply and let go of all tension or anxiety. As you relax, you find yourself in a deep, quiet place inside. Allow yourself to just rest in that place for a few moments, with nothing you need to do or think about.

From this deep, quiet place, begin to sense the life force within you. Imagine that you are following your own energy, feeling it, trusting it, moving with it in every moment of your life. You are being completely true to yourself, speaking and living your truth. You feel alive and empowered. Imagine that you are expressing your creativity fully and freely, and let yourself enjoy that experience. By being who you are and expressing yourself, you are having a healing and empowering effect on everyone you encounter and on the world around you.

# Exploring Our Many Selves

One of the difficulties in learning to trust and follow our intuitive "voice" is that we have many different voices or energies within us, and often they are all feeling and saying different and contradictory things! This can be quite confusing. With practice and awareness, we can learn to distinguish the energy of our intuition from any other. In fact, it usually has its own distinct feeling.

Discovering some of the many other inner voices or selves within us, however, can be useful and important. If we can become aware of who is "talking" to us or directing us internally, we can begin to have much more consciousness and choice in our lives.

Practice in listening inside will help you to decipher what your gut feeling is telling you and to sort out all the other voices inside of you. As you begin to pay more attention to your internal dialogues, you will become more familiar with the varying qualities of the different selves.

For example, you may notice that a certain voice inside of you has a judging, critical quality — it's always pointing out what you did wrong. That is your inner *critic*. Another voice might always be telling you what you "should" be doing — that's probably your inner *authoritarian* or your *pusher*.

It's important to notice that your higher power, coming through your intuition, never speaks in harsh, judgmental, or tyrannical ways. Its tone is encouraging and supportive, and it usually brings a feeling of aliveness and empowerment or comfort and serenity. Following its guidance will not result in pressure, tension, or self-doubt, but in expanded awareness and energy.

There are an infinite number of different selves within us, and each person has a different configuration. Some common ones that you may come to recognize within yourself might be:

| | |
|---|---|
| The Perfectionist | The Vulnerable Child |
| The Critic or Judge | The Playful Child |
| The Mother or Father | The Adolescent |
| The Pusher | The Rebel |
| The Rational Mind | The Creative Artist |
| The Rescuer | The Victim |
| The Spiritual Seeker | The Hedonist |

You may discover some of these or others while doing the meditations.

If you give each of these voices a chance to speak, you will be more able to distinguish them from your intuitive voice. This next exercise is designed to help you do that. You may want to do it with a friend so that one of you can read the meditation while the other experiences it. Or, you can record it in your own voice and then do the exercise as you play it back.

## EXERCISE 9

### *Meditation*

Sit or lie down in a comfortable position in a quiet place. Close your eyes and relax. Take several slow, deep breaths, relaxing your body more with each breath. Relax your mind and let your thoughts drift away. Try not to attach yourself to any one thought. As each thought comes into your mind, let it go.

Now imagine you are walking down a beautiful spiral staircase . . . descending further and further with each step. When you come to the base of the staircase, you find a huge door in front of you. Open it up and walk into a large, majestic room with a round table and chairs in it. Take time to explore the room. When you are ready, choose a chair, sit down, and be comfortable. Sit quietly for a while, allowing your mind to become calm and clear. Then gradually start listening for those parts of your personality that want to speak out. When you become aware of one voice as louder than the others, have that part of you take a seat at the table. Let this voice say everything it needs to say. It may be your critical voice that wants to tell you everything you've been doing wrong, or perhaps it's a frightened part of you that wants to describe how frightened he or she is. It may want to talk about one issue or problem in your life, or it may want to discuss your life in general. Let the voice express any thoughts or feelings it has.

As the voice is speaking, other parts of you may begin to react. For example, while your critical voice has the floor, your rebel or your frightened child may also want to speak. Allow these voices to take a chair, in turn, giving each the opportunity to have a say. The entire table may be filled with different parts of you before all opinions and feelings have been expressed. Try not to figure anything out; just allow the different energies and voices to speak. Take as much time as you need to let each communicate with you. When they have finished speaking, acknowledge each one for what he or she has given you.

After all the voices have spoken, take a few minutes to observe them and acknowledge them as the many parts of your personality. When you feel ready, prepare yourself to move into a deeper level of your being. Imagine yourself leaving the table and walking toward a tunnel. As you enter the tunnel, you notice that it is lit by a beautiful light. As you walk through this tunnel, you absorb this healing light and become aware that the voices grow fainter behind you. This is a magical tunnel that is leading you to a safe, beautiful place. With each step, you get nearer to your inner sanctuary. Soon the tunnel opens up and you are there. What does your sanctuary look and feel like? Create it exactly the way you want it, indoors or outdoors, a place you've been before, or a place you make up right now.

Find a comfortable place to sit or lie down in your sanctuary and breathe deeply until you are relaxed and at peace.

Now focus on your conscious awareness on the deep place in your body where your inner being or higher power resides. Let your intuitive self come forward. Does it have anything to tell you — a message for you? Feel free to talk to your intuition, to make requests or ask questions. Is there anything you want to ask your intuition right now? Ask and relax. Keep your mind free of thoughts and open to receiving the answers. Spend as much time as you want with your intuition. Then, when you are ready, thank your intuition for guidance.

Imagine another tunnel that leads you out of your inner sanctuary and back into the room you presently are in. When you come back to the room, slowly become aware of the sounds around you, your feet or body on the ground, and the feeling of the room. Whenever you're ready, simply open your eyes.

In the space below (and on the following page), you may want to record the various voices you experienced and summarize the feelings or ideas each one expressed. Then, describe your inner sanctuary and your experience with contacting your intuition. What was the basic feeling or message you got?

We are all born with an infinite number of different qualities or energies within us. One of our most important tasks in life is to discover and develop as many of these energies as possible so that we can be well-rounded and experience the full range of our potential.

We can think of these energies as different archetypes, subpersonalities, or selves within us. In a way, it's as if there are many different characters living inside of us, each with its own task and purpose.

Since the physical world is a plane of duality, for each of these energies within us, there is an opposite energy. In order to experience wholeness and balance, we need to develop and integrate both sides of every polarity.

Most of us, however, are not accustomed to thinking in this way. We have been taught to think in a linear, exclusive fashion — good/bad, right/wrong. So if one quality is good or desirable, its opposite is bad, or undesirable.

For example, many of us have been taught that it is virtuous and admirable to give to others; a person who gives a lot is a good person. Therefore, taking is thought to be selfish; a person who takes a lot for himself might be judged as less worthy than a giving person.

Someone else with different values might think of this in an opposite way — admiring a person who knows how to take for himself and considering that person to be smart and successful while looking down on someone who is less aggressive and more giving as being foolish and easily taken advantage of.

Either way, one polarity is honored while the opposite is devalued. In reality, both giving and receiving are equally important and valuable. In fact, we are often in desperate need of these hidden qualities in order to bring healing and balance into our lives.

From the time we are born, we begin to experiment with expressing the different energies within us. At that time we are completely dependent on our parents or caretakers for our survival, so we are sensitive to their reactions to us. Expressing one energy might invoke approval and positive attention while expressing another energy draws disapproval and often times rejection. Soon, we have a good sense of which energies help us get our needs met.

As we grow up, we continue to develop the energies that seem to work best to meet our needs. We become identified with these qualities; that's who we think we are. These dominant energies become our *primary selves* — the inner characters whose job it is to take care of us and make our lives work as well as possible.

For every primary self, there is an opposite energy, which has often been repressed or denied because one way or another we got the message that it was not okay, or because it simply hasn't had space to develop. These energies become our *disowned selves*. They are usually buried within our psyche and we either don't know about them at all, or we are aware of them and try to hide them from the world. The disowned selves make up our shadow side, the parts of ourselves that we are embarrassed about, ashamed of, fearful of, or uncomfortable with. Our primary selves are usually working hard to make sure that we don't show these disowned selves to the world, since they are convinced that this would invite criticism, rejection, abandonment, or some form of disaster.

The problem is that each of these disowned selves carries an essential energy that is an important part of us. In fact, we are often in desperate need of these qualities in order to bring healing and balance into our lives. For example, many of us are very identified with being strong and self-sufficient and we disown the part of us that feels vulnerable and has needs. Yet our vulnerable side is the sensitive part of us that can allow us to receive love, and to experience intimacy with others.

So, how do we become conscious of the many selves within and bring them into balance?

The first and most important step is to begin to recognize and become aware of your primary selves. What qualities and energies are you most identified with? Begin with a list of characteristics that best describe you. For example: hard working, shy, powerful, or creative. We want to honor and appreciate our primary selves for how much they've done for us while separating from being totally identified with them. As soon as we become conscious of them as energies within us rather than who we are, we are beginning to develop what is called *aware ego.*\* Aware ego is the ability to recognize and hold all the different selves within us, so that we can have conscious choice about which ones we bring through at any given moment.

Once we have some awareness in relation to our primary selves, the second step is to increase our awareness of the disowned or denied aspects of ourselves.

## Exercise 10

Make a list of your primary characteristics or selves in the first column, and then make a second list, writing down the qualities you consider to be the opposite of those in the first list. An example follows:

| *List #1* | *List #2* |
|---|---|
| *Primary characteristics* | *Opposite characteristics* |
| *hard working* | *lazy* |
| *strong* | *weak* |
| *caring* | *selfish* |
| *responsible* | *irresponsible* |
| 1. | 1. |
| 2. | 2. |
| 3. | 3. |
| 4. | 4. |
| 5. | 5. |

\* Aware ego is a term created by Drs. Hal and Sidra Stone from their renowned model, the Psychology of Selves, featuring the Voice Dialogue method.

When you've finished, rewrite your second list using terms that might be considered less judgmental or more open-minded, but still reflect the essence of the descriptive word you've used. For example, a revised List #2 might look like this:

| List #1 | List #2 | List #2 Revised |
| --- | --- | --- |
| Primary characteristics | Opposite characteristics | Less judgmental opposite characteristics |
| hardworking | lazy | relaxed |
| strong | weak | vulnerable/receptive |
| caring | selfish | caring for self |
| responsible | irresponsible | carefree |
| 1. | 1. | 1. |
| 2. | 2. | 2. |
| 3. | 3. | 3. |
| 4. | 4. | 4. |
| 5. | 5. | 5. |

Sometimes it may be very difficult to translate these terms and find an acceptable synonym. Embracing our denied self or shadow side is a complex (and necessary) process and these exercises are merely an introduction to that process. (As noted earlier, other books that I have written, including *Living in the Light,* delve more deeply into this process.)

## EXERCISE 11

When you've completed your lists, take each set of opposing energies, and in one column, list some rules and expectations your hard working primary self has dictated to you. In the other column, record your relaxed opposite self's reactions to each demand.

For example:

*Hard Working*

*I can't go on a nature hike until I've completed all of my work.*

*Relaxed*

*Relaxing is important. It allows more creativity to flow and I actually get more accomplished in my work.*

---

*Column 1*

1.

2.

3.

*Column 2*

1.

2.

3.

| *Column 1* | *Column 2* |
|---|---|
| 4. | 4. |
| 5. | 5. |

## EXERCISE 12

Close your eyes and allow images of these selves you've been working with to form in your mind's eye. Again, if you don't see a clear picture, try to get a feeling or sense of what they are like. Once you have formed some impression, listen to what they have to say.

Next, in writing, describe each of these polarities, giving them form. You may want to give them each a name and have them talk with each other. If you like, you can create pictures of them, too. Do this exercise with each set of polarities that you have discovered.

Making peace with our selves means acknowledging and appreciating all aspects of who we are. True "consciousness" involves holding both sides of any polarity, not identifying with one. Exploring and embracing our many selves is the only path toward truly "living in the light."

For more complete information on this fascinating topic, read *Embracing Our Selves* by Drs. Hal and Sidra Stone, Nataraj/New World Library, 1989. Or listen to their tapes, available through Delos, Inc., P.O. Box 604, Albion, CA 95410.

# The World
# As Our Mirror

The physical world is our creation: we each create our own version of the world, our particular reality, our unique life experience. Because I am creating my life, I can look at my creation to get feedback about myself. Just as an artist looks at his latest creation to see what works well and what doesn't, and thereby improves his skills, we can look at the ongoing masterwork of our lives to appreciate who we are and to recognize what we still need to learn.

We're creating our lives as we go along; therefore, our experiences give us an instant, ongoing reflection of ourselves. In fact, the external world is like a giant mirror that reflects our consciousness clearly and accurately. Once we have learned how to look into that mirror and perceive and interpret its reflection, we have a fabulous tool for self-awareness.

Understanding that the world is our mirror can help us see our lives as a reflection of our beliefs, attitudes, and emotional patterns. Viewed in this way, the external world can teach us about hidden aspects of ourselves that we can't see directly. The process is based on two premises:

1. I assume that *everything* in my life is my reflection, my creation; there are no accidents or events that are unrelated to me. If I see or feel something, if it has any impact on me, then my soul has attracted or created it to show me something. If it didn't mirror some part of myself, I wouldn't even

be able to see it. All the people in my life are reflections of the various characters and energies that live inside of me.

2. I always try to avoid putting myself down for the reflections I see. I know that nothing is negative. Everything is a gift that brings me to self-awareness — after all, I'm here to learn. If I was already perfect I wouldn't be here. Why should I get angry at myself when I see things I've been unconscious of? It would be like a first grader getting frustrated because she wasn't in college yet. I try to maintain a compassionate attitude toward myself and my learning process. To the extent that I can do this, the learning process becomes fun and really quite interesting.

I am learning to view my life as a fascinating and adventurous movie. All the characters in it are parts of me played out on the big screen so that I can clearly see them. Once I see them and recognize their various feelings and voices inside myself, I can understand that they are all important and valuable parts of me that I need for my full expression in this life.

If the movie portrays problems, hassles, or struggles, I know I must check inside to find out where I'm not being true to myself or have more learning and healing to do. I also know that when I'm trusting and being myself as fully as possible, everything in my life reflects this by falling into place easily and working smoothly.

Those newly introduced to the concept of mirroring may often see something mirrored in their life they don't like and then blame themselves. If you find yourself reacting this way, remember that the universe does not offer us a tool of enlightenment so we can beat ourselves with it. Treat yourself with love and compassion, as you would a child who is eager to learn.

The most important key in changing the outside world is understanding how what we feel and believe is reflected outside us. Once we shed light on a process that has been unconscious, it will no longer run our lives without our knowledge. We will regain power over what happens to us.

The following exercises on mirroring are intended to help you uncover your unconscious beliefs and guide you in learning to treat yourself better. As you complete the exercises, you will begin to see clearly the changes you have made reflected in the world around you.

Remember, in using the mirroring process it's important to:

1. Assume that everything in your life is your reflection, your creation. No accidents or events are unrelated to you.

2. Avoid putting yourself down for the reflections you see. Nothing is negative; every reflection is a gift that brings awareness. After all, we are here to learn. If we were already perfect, we wouldn't need to be here.

## EXERCISE 13

Focus on a particular incident in your life that is troubling you. In the space below, briefly describe the problem. Then, ask yourself how this mirrors your feelings. Write down the response. Some examples follow. (There is space for you to focus on other incidents later, if you'd like.)

1. **Problem:** *My boss criticizes any new ideas I have. He seems opposed to innovative ideas.*
   **Mirror:** *I always doubt any new ideas I have. I tell myself they're not good enough. I'm afraid of change.*

2. **Problem:** *One of my closest friends said she felt I had no time for her and that she was a nuisance to me.*
   **Mirror:** *I have no time for myself. I have not valued my feelings and needs lately.*

3. **Problem:** *My boss got angry at me for being late several times this week.*
   **Mirror:** *I have dreaded going into work. I have been angry at myself for continuing to work at a job I can't stand.*

1.

2.

3.

4.

5.

6.

7.

8.

9.

10.

Once you discover how an external problem actually mirrors what's going on inside of you, try not to blame yourself. Instead, when you realize that something you have been doing to yourself is causing harmful results, ask the universe for help. You can say to your higher power, "Show me what I need to know about this," or "Help me find consciousness and healing in this part of my life."

## EXERCISE 14

We often can see a direct correlation between how we treat ourselves and how others treat us. In the first column, write down all the things you did or said in the last week that were positive or supportive of yourself. Then, in the second column, list the ways this self-nurturing was mirrored by positive events. Some examples follow.

| *What I Did for Myself* | *Mirror* |
|---|---|
| *I wrote self-esteem affirmations; I took a hot bath and meditated; bought myself a beautiful scarf; I called Joe to ask about possible speaking engagements; played tennis; fixed myself a delicious and healthy dinner; I asked a co-worker for help with a project; went camping with my family; took myself to my favorite restaurant for lunch; reorganized my desk and threw out everything I didn't need; put flowers on my desk* | *Two people commented that I looked beautiful today; found a five-dollar bill; felt healthy and energetic; got a letter from my parents with lots of good news; Bill called and asked me out; my boss said he liked my work; got more than I expected in my tax return; was invited to speak at a conference.* |

1.


2.


3.

| *What I Did for Myself* | *Mirror* |
| --- | --- |

4.

5.

6.

7.

8.

9.

10.

## EXERCISE 15

Reflect on the different categories of your life — work and career, relationships, money, sexuality, body, home environment. What is the statement (or major event as shown in example #2) that reflects your attitude about each? Write it down in the "mirror" column. Then describe how this reflects your internal belief system in the "belief" column. If you identify a limiting or negative belief, turn it into an affirmation. Write the affirmation below this negative belief. (There is space for you to add other events later, if you'd like.)

| *Mirror* | *Belief/Affirmation* |
|---|---|
| **WORK AND CAREER** | |
| **Examples:** | |
| *1. I have a great job that I love to do, but I make a minimal income.* | *I don't believe I can make money doing what I love to do.* |
| | **Affirmation:** *I now make a good income doing what I love to do.* |
| *2. I was fired from my job and I don't know what to do next.* | *I was no longer feeling fulfilled in that job and I wanted to leave but I was afraid to lose the security.* |
| | **Affirmation:** *I am being guided, step by step, to work that is right for me.* |
| 1. | |
| 2. | |

|                     _Mirror_                     |           _Belief/Affirmation_           |
| ------------------------------------------------ | ---------------------------------------- |

3.



4.



5.



## RELATIONSHIPS

### Examples:

1. *I'm always attracted to women who turn out to be emotional and needy.*

   *I'm afraid of my own emotions and my need. It would embarrass me to show the vulnerable side of me so I repress it, and the women in my life act it out.*

   **Affirmation:** *It's okay for me to have emotions and needs. To accept my vulnerability makes me a stronger person. I can share my strength and vulnerability with a strong and vulnerable partner.*

| *Mirror* | *Belief/Affirmation* |
|---|---|
| 2. *I want a lasting relationship but I can't seem to find someone who wants to make a commitment.* | *I'm afraid to be really committed to myself in a relationship. I always try to please the other person and lose my sense of myself.* |
| | **Affirmation:** *I am committed to being honest and real in a relationship. I have a strong committed relationship with myself. I am attracting a wonderful* |

1.

2.

3.

| _Mirror_ | _Belief/Affirmation_ |
|---|---|

4.


5.


**MONEY**

**Examples:**

1. *I never have enough money for anything pleasurable or fun, just enough to pay the bills.*

   *My parents always had the bare minimum. I feel guilty having extra money.*

   **Affirmation:** *It's okay for me to have more money than my parents. It's good for me to have money for pleasure and fun. I deserve to have pleasure in my life. I now have enough money to enjoy myself.*

2. *Money does not come easily.*

   *I always have to work hard and really push myself to earn a living. Life is a struggle to survive.*

   **Affirmation:** *Life is fulfilling and enjoyable. Money comes to me easily as I do what I love.*

|  | _Mirror_ | _Belief/Affirmation_ |
|---|---|---|

1.

2.

3.

4.

5.

| *Mirror* | *Belief/Affirmation* |
|---|---|

**SEXUALITY**

**Examples:**

1. *I love my wife but I don't have much energy for sex lately. Our sexual relationship seems dull and dead.*

   *I'm afraid to express a lot of my feelings and emotions, especially my anger and my fear, for fear my wife will leave me or reject me. I'm deadening myself to a lot of my feelings and my sexual energy reflects that.*

   **Affirmation:** *It's important for me to express my feelings. The more I express my feelings, the more I am loved. I am now expressing my feelings freely and responsibly.*

2. *I only feel passionate around emotionally unavailable men. The others bore me.*

   *My father didn't want me — who does? There must be something wrong with me.*

   **Affirmation:** *I am now willing to feel passionate about men who want me. I am worth wanting. I deserve to be loved. I am attracting wonderful, loving, sexy, emotionally available men into my life.*

|            *Mirror*            |        *Belief/Affirmation*        |
| --- | --- |

1.

2.

3.

4.

5.

| *Mirror* | *Belief/Affirmation* |
|---|---|

**BODY**

**Examples:**

1. *I am overweight and no matter how much I diet, I can't seem to keep the weight off.*

*I don't believe I have a right to take up space. I have trouble asserting myself and asking for what I want or setting boundaries with those I love. My body is reacting by taking up the extra "space" that I deny myself emotionally.*

**Affirmation:** *I have a right to take up space. I ask for what I want. It's okay for me to say "no" to people when I want to. I take care of myself and trust others to take care of themselves. I am a strong, assertive, healthy, attractive person.*

2. *I'm tired a lot and I have a lot of minor physical symptoms.*

*I believe that my worth hinges on how much I do, so I push myself all the time to do as much as possible. Resting and relaxing make me feel guilty.*

**Affirmation:** *I deserve to rest, relax, and nurture myself. My body deserves to be loved and taken care of. Just by being who I am, I am worthy and lovable.*

|               | *Mirror*                  | *Belief/Affirmation* |
|---------------|---------------------------|----------------------|

1.

2.

3.

4.

5.

| *Mirror* | *Belief/Affirmation* |
|---|---|

**HOME ENVIRONMENT**

**Examples:**

*1. My home is too small and cramped. I feel closed in when I'm there.*

*I'm afraid to admit how expansive and powerful I really am and how big my visions are. I'm holding myself back and limiting myself.*

**Affirmation:** *I am powerful, creative, and unlimited. I am creating a spacious, attractive home for myself.*

*2. I want to move but can't find a place at a price I can afford.*

*I don't believe there's a nice place to live within my price range.*

**Affirmation:** *I am now living in a wonderful home that I can easily afford.*

1.


2.

3.



4.



5.



Note: As you can see from the examples, our core negative beliefs are often entwined with deep emotional issues. Identifying these beliefs and issues and doing affirmations can be very helpful, but it is not a substitute for good professional therapy. I recommend seeking support from a good therapist with experience in the specific issue that is troubling you.

# The Male and Female Within

Each of us has male and female energies within us. Our female energy is the intuitive self — the deep, wise, guiding aspect of ourselves. Feminine energy is receptive, thus it forms the channel through which our higher self moves to connect with us. Our female speaks to us through inner promptings, gut feelings, or images that arise out of a deep place within us. When we do not listen to the voice of our intuition, the female energy within us will often communicate through dreams or emotions, or through our physical condition.

Our male aspect takes action in the world. It enables us to *do* things — to build, to speak, to move our bodies. Where the female within is receptive, our male energies are assertive, outgoing, and expressive. It is the male within us that brings ideas into being, transforms thought into form.

Female intuition plus male action equals creativity. The feminine is the source of creative inspiration and the masculine implements her vision. The interplay of these energies within us is the vehicle for the creative energy of the universe to channel through us. So, the more in tune with each aspect we are, the more easily we are able to listen to and act on the voice of our intuition.

In the next few exercises, you will meet your inner female and male. They will help you discover your goals and visions and make these visions a reality.

In the following meditation, trust the images or feelings that come when you ask to see your inner male and female. One or both could be people you actually know, archetypal or fantasy figures, or they could appear in the form of an animal. Accept what comes. If you do the meditation more than once, they may be different each time.

## EXERCISE 16

### *Meditation*

Sit or lie down in a comfortable position and close your eyes. Take a few deep breaths and allow your body and mind to relax completely. Then, gradually move your conscious awareness into a quiet place within you.

Now visualize an image that represents your inner female. This image could be an actual or imaginary person, an animal, or even something abstract such as a color or shape. Accept whatever arises spontaneously in your mind.

Look closely at your female image and try to sense or feel what she represents to you. Notice the image's details, her colors and textures, and be aware of how you feel about her.

After you have established a sense of rapport with your female image, ask her if she has anything she would like to say to you right now. Allow yourself to receive her communication in whatever form it may come, whether in words, feelings, or images. If you have any questions for her, ask them. Again, be open to reply in any form.

Once you have received her communication, and you feel complete for the moment, take a deep breath and release her image from your mind. Come back to a quiet, still place.

Now, draw to mind an image that represents your male self. Again, accept whatever image comes to you. It could be a man, a boy, an animal, or some abstract symbol or color. Slowly explore this image as well, noting all details, colors, and textures. Become aware of how you feel about him; then, ask if he has anything to say to you at this time. Be receptive to his communication, whatever its form. If you have anything you want to ask him, do this now. Accept whatever words, feelings, or images you may receive. If an answer doesn't come to you immediately, know that it will come later.

Once you feel complete with your communication with him, release the male image from your mind and return to a quiet place inside.

Now ask that both your male and female appear to you at the same time.

Observe them together. Do they relate to one another or are they separate? If they do relate to one another, how do they relate? Ask them if they have anything they would like to communicate to one another. Stay open to what comes to you in words, images, or feelings. If you have anything you'd like to say to them or ask them, do that now.

When you feel complete, once again take a deep breath and release their images from your mind. Return to a quiet, still place inside before ending this exercise. Take a few deep breaths and open your eyes, feeling refreshed and revitalized. With crayons, paint, or colored pens, create a picture of your inner male and female images and/or write about your experiences with them.

*Meditation*

This meditation show us the power of having a male that supports our female.

Close your eyes and get in touch with your female intuitive voice.

Ask her if she wants anything. Is there a gift she desires or something she wants to say or do? When she has told you what she wants, visualize your new male supporting her desire and taking whatever action is necessary to honor her request.

Be aware of how this feels to you.

## EXERCISE 18

In the left column, list everything you (your female) wants, and in the right column, list what you (your male) can do to give you (your female) what you want.

In doing this exercise, it's important not to attempt to do too much, otherwise you may begin to feel overwhelmed. Limit your list to one or two things at a time. This will build the trust between your female and male. (There is space for you to come back and add more if you wish.)

| *Female* | *Male* |
|---|---|
| *(What You Want)* | *(What You Can Do to Give Yourself What You Want)* |

**Examples:**

| | |
|---|---|
| *1. More rest.* | *Put on soft music and lie down for ten minutes.* |
| *2. Paint.* | *Purchase paints and canvas, and paint at least one hour this week.* |
| *3. Eat more healthful food.* | *Stop at the health food store or farmer's market and buy pleasing, healthful fruits, vegetables, and grains. Using a whole foods cookbook, create a simple, visually stimulating, and nutritious meal.* |
| *4. Go back to work in business again.* | *Make three phone calls to explore job possibilities.* |
| *5. Travel and adventure — see new places.* | *Get posters and travel brochures of exciting places. Hang them on the wall and begin visualizing traveling there.* |

| *Female* | *Male* |
|---|---|
| (*What You Want*) | (*What You Can Do to Give Yourself What You Want*) |

1.


2.


3.


4.


5.

| *Female* | *Male* |
|---|---|
| (What You Want) | (What You Can Do to Give Yourself What You Want) |

6.

7.

8.

9.

10.

# Spirit and Form

Our spirit is the creative energy of the universe, and it moves through us to manifest in the world. Our form is our physical body, our mind, and our personality — the medium through which our spirit moves. Although neither spirit nor form could exist apart from one another in this physical world, until we learn to listen to and trust our intuition, our spirit and form will often conflict. While our spirit yearns for greater life, energy, change, and inner fulfillment, our form seeks safety and security and fears risk or change.

As young children, the channels between our spirit and form are relatively open, but as we grow older and learn to shun our intuitive awareness (spirit) in favor of more conventional behavior that conforms to the world around us (form), these channels become blocked. We lose touch with our spirit and forget our purpose for being here. We lose sight of the creative goals and spiritual ideals that come from our spirit. Form becomes paramount, yet our spirit still seeks expression. Thus, we feel dissatisfied and out of balance.

Even though we may enjoy some amount of material success, we are still not happy. In an effort to restore balance, we urgently seek gratification — through greater material success, or superficial relationships, or even through various means of escape such as drugs or alcohol. But because we don't understand the true cause of our dissatisfaction — our lack of connection to our spirit — all of our efforts fail. Gradually, we succumb to hopelessness.

Yet in this very hopelessness lies our greatest hope, for when we are hopeless, we give up — we give up our attachment to the way we've been doing things, and release old behaviors and old forms from our lives. At this point, the channel to our spirit can be re-opened, if we are guided to listen for the voice of our spirit, our intuition. Our spirit, with all its creative energy and intense drive, is waiting to fill the void in our lives, to provide us with the satisfaction and balance we have been seeking.

The following exercise helps reveal the distance and degree of conflict between form and spirit that now exist in you, and suggests actions you can take to bring your form and spirit into alignment.

## EXERCISE 19

In the first column below, list several examples of consistent fantasies you have about things you want to do, how you want to live, or ways in which you want to express yourself. In the next column, describe what your form is actually doing in relation to this. In the third column, create a step you can take now to respond to and support your spirit through your form. For some of you, this may entail taking a physical step into the world, such as following a job lead, trying out for a part in a play, or writing affirmations. For others, this step could be lying in bed, meditating, or learning to love and nurture yourself in some other way.

| *Spirit* | *Form* | *Action* |
|---|---|---|
| *What I desire to do:* | *What I am now doing:* | *One step I can take toward expressing my desire:* |

**Examples:**

| | | |
|---|---|---|
| *1. Write a novel* | *I'm now working as a copy editor at a local paper* | *Begin writing creatively one hour a week just for fun* |
| *2. Live in a beautiful, secluded home by the water* | *I'm living in a dumpy apartment in the city* | *Talk to a friend about sharing expenses for a more pleasant apartment with a nice yard. Take a step in the right direction* |
| *3. Wake people up about the importance of environmental/ ecological issues* | *Nothing* | *Join an environmental activist group and pledge a few hours or a few dollars a month toward helping* |

| Spirit | Form | Action |
|--------|------|--------|
| *What I desire to do:* | *What I am now doing:* | *One step I can take toward expressing my desire:* |

1.

2.

3.

4.

5.

| *Spirit* | *Form* | *Action* |
|---|---|---|
| *What I desire to do:* | *What I am now doing:* | *One step I can take toward expressing my desire:* |

6.

7.

8.

9.

10.

## EXERCISE 20

*Meditation*

Get comfortable, relax, and close your eyes. Take a few deep breaths and relax your body and mind completely. Allow your conscious awareness to move into a deep, quiet place within you.

Imagine that there is a beautiful golden light radiating from a place deep within you. It begins to grow and expand until it fills your entire body. It's very powerful, and as it fills you, it penetrates into every cell of your body, literally waking up each molecule to the light. Imagine your entire body glowing and radiating with this light. Then, see and feel your body being transformed — becoming healthier, stronger, and more beautiful. Imagine everything else in your life being similarly transformed.

# Authoritarian and Rebel

The authoritarian and the rebel are two parts of the personality that many of us have in one form or another. If they are strong voices in us, they can make it difficult to sense and follow our intuition. If we are unconscious of them, they may control our behavior in a way that interferes with our ability to get in touch with our true desires. The battle between them can create tremendous conflict within us, as well.

As in dealing with all of our inner selves, the first and most important step is becoming conscious of them. Once we become aware of them, we are already separating from being identified with them. We recognize them as part of us, and we begin to have conscious choice about how much power we give them. We can appreciate them for the ways in which they've tried to help us, and for what they still have to offer us.

The inner authoritarian carries our need for order and structure and the rules we have learned about how we should behave. People who grow up in a home with a strong authoritarian parent figure, or in a very authoritarian religion, always develop a powerful inner authoritarian self who carries all the values and rules of the external authority figures. It tries to protect you and keep you safe by making sure that you follow the rules, maintain order, and behave as a good, responsible person.

If you have a strong authoritarian self, you usually make one of two choices: you strive to follow its rules, or you rebel against them. If you follow them faithfully, you are likely to be a responsible, law-abiding person and oftentimes a high achiever. You may, however, lose touch with your spontaneous, free-spirited, creative energies and, eventually, you may even feel that you've lost your soul.

Some people react to their authoritarian upbringing and their own internalized authoritarian by developing a strong rebellious self. They become identified with the rebel and disown the authoritarian self, but it remains in the shadow of their unconscious, trying to control their behavior and constantly triggering the rebel into action.

The rebel usually develops in childhood or adolescence, in an attempt to maintain a sense of self and find some freedom in an overly oppressive rule structure. This can literally be a life saver at the time. Unfortunately, the rebel is just a knee-jerk reaction to the authoritarian's rules. It reacts in rebellion to any controlling influence from inside or out. It will automatically do the opposite of whatever it thinks it's supposed to do.

As always, when we are overly identified with an energy, we attract its opposite in our relationships. Whether we become overly identified with the authoritarian or with the rebel, these identifications are unconscious, so there is no real choice or freedom. When your authoritarian self is dictating your every move, or is constantly battling with your rebel, it is almost impossible to get in touch with your intuitive feelings or true desires.

## EXERCISE 21

This exercise can help you identify some of your authoritarian and rebel behaviors. In the first column, list some rules and expectations your authoritarian has dictated to you. In the second column, record your rebel's reactions to each demand. Some examples follow.

| *Authoritarian* | *Rebel* |
|---|---|
| 1. *You have to work all the time to be successful. Work, work, work. You're lazy! Get up and do something!* | *That's a lie. I don't have to listen to you, you slave driver. Creative geniuses need time at the beach (or the bar or wherever). I really don't feel like doing anything at all!* |
| 2. *Stop eating all that food. You're fat. Nobody's going to want you. You'd better start dieting right away.* | *I don't care what you or anybody else thinks. I'm going to do what I want. I'll eat whatever I want.* |

|                | _Authoritarian_ | _Rebel_ |
| -------------- | --------------- | ------- |
| 1.             |                 |         |
| 2.             |                 |         |
| 3.             |                 |         |
| 4.             |                 |         |
| 5.             |                 |         |

|   | *Authoritarian* | *Rebel* |
|---|---|---|

6.

7.

8.

9.

10.

## EXERCISE 22

*Meditation*

Close your eyes and allow images of your authoritarian and rebel to form in your mind's eye. If you don't see a clear picture, try to get a feeling or sense of what they are like. Once you have formed some impression, listen to what they have to say.

Next, in writing, describe your authoritarian and rebel, giving them full color and form. You may want to give them each a name and have them talk with each other. If you like, use your colored pencils to create pictures of them, too.

**Example:**

*My authoritarian is a huge woman. She wears a black miniskirt and boots. She carries a whip. She's constantly giving orders and making demands, and she expects to be obeyed. Her name is Bertha.*

*My rebel lies on the beach, smokes cigarettes, and eats chocolates all day long. Her name is Billie. She gazes endlessly out over the ocean and has no cares or concerns about the day.*

*Billie does not want to hear what Bertha says, so she ignores her. Bertha hates this, so she gets bigger, louder, and angrier. Then Billie thumbs her nose at Bertha. An so it goes, on and on.*

**Another example:**

*My authoritarian is my father. He's very rational and very convincing in his explanations about the "right" way to live and how important it is to get ahead professionally and financially. He insists that I go back to college for my master's degree so I can achieve more professional success.*

*My rebel wears a black leather jacket and is totally uninterested in education or career. He just wants to ride a motorcycle, chase women, and do whatever feels good. He just ignores the father part.*

After describing the interaction between your authoritarian and your rebel, close your eyes and visualize the two of them stuck in their positions. When the image is clearer, move away from them, and allow an image or feeling of your higher self or your intuitive wisdom to appear. Listen to what this part has to say to you. Then describe this in writing.

Example:

*When I move away from my authoritarian and rebel, I see an image of a wise old man in a monk's habit. He is seated on a rock in the middle of a beautiful meadow. He tells me that he has always been with me and will continue to be here when I am willing to come to him. He says the authoritarian and rebel are both aspects of me, but neither one is who I really am. He can help me get in touch with a deeper sense of myself.*

# Daily Life

In this section, we will learn how to live the principles we've been learning by applying them to the practical, everyday concerns of life: money, work, play, health, body image, relationships, sexuality, and children. As you follow your inner guidance and apply it to these concerns, you will move toward aliveness, health, prosperity, and creativity.

# Feelings

Many of us have not learned how to experience or express our feelings. Until very recently, our families and society have not placed much value on feelings or their expression. Because of this, we often overlook our own feelings. The energy of these unfelt, unexpressed feelings remains blocked in our bodies where it can cause emotional and physical discomfort and, eventually, illness and disease.

Many people are afraid to experience their so-called "negative" emotions — sadness, hurt, anger, fear, or despair. They are afraid they will be overwhelmed by these emotions if they open up to them, or they may fear they will be stuck with these negative feelings forever.

Actually the opposite is true: When you are willing to fully experience a particular feeling, the blocked energy will be released and the feeling will dissolve.

The problem is, when people are uncomfortable or in pain, they don't know how to do this. We are in the habit of going about our lives simply hoping this discomfort or pain will go away.

We need to begin to give our feelings priority. We can learn how to acknowledge our feelings and give them the expression they deserve. If we do this regularly, we need never get to the point where our pain paralyzes us with fear. The following exercises can assist you in this process.

## EXERCISE 23

### *Meditation*

Close your eyes and focus your attention on the middle of your body — on your heart, your solar plexus, and your abdomen. Ask yourself how you are feeling emotionally right now. Try to distinguish the feelings from the thoughts you are having in your head. Are you feeling peaceful, excited, anxious, sad, angry, empty, joyful, frustrated, guilty, loving, lonely, fulfilled, serious, or playful?

If you find an unhappy or upset feeling inside of you, go into that feeling and give it a voice. Ask it to talk to you and tell you what it's feeling. Try to listen carefully to its point of view. Be sympathetic, loving, and supportive toward your feelings. Ask if there is anything you can do to take better care of yourself. Use the space below to record any aspects of this dialogue you may wish to remember.

## EXERCISE 24

For this exercise, you will need colored pens, or crayons, or even finger paints. Whichever medium you decide to use, put it in front of you on a clear table with plenty of space. Have plenty of large sheets of unlined white paper available. Now take a deep breath, and notice how you feel. Are you feeling tired, anxious, happy? What color is the feeling? Pick the color from among your pens, crayons or paints that represents your feeling. Start to draw with that color, using either your dominant or nondominant hand, or both. What shape is the feeling? (Trust your impulse about this.) Use the color you've chosen and any other colors you want to draw a picture of how you are feeling — literal or abstract. Sit and look at your drawing for a while. Keep following any impulses you have to add to the drawing, using any colors and shapes that feel right to you. Don't worry about how it looks or what it means, just do what you feel. When your drawing "feels" complete, turn the paper over. Use a crayon to write three words that describe your drawing(s). Notice how you are feeling now. This exercise is not an attempt to change your feelings. It is a way of learning to accept, experience, and express your feelings. Do this exercise as often as you want.

## EXERCISE 25

Moving your body, making sound, and breathing allows the body to release unexpressed emotion.

Even if you don't know how you're feeling or don't feel you have any-thing to release, you can do the following exercise. Be sure to notice how you feel after completing it and take the time to write down anything you may feel was significant while you did the exercise.

Stand in a comfortable position with your feet shoulder-length apart. Take several deep breaths, and as you inhale stretch you hands above your head. As you exhale, drop your hands to the floor, bending your body at the waist. Repeat this process several times, and as you inhale, imagine you're scooping energy up from the earth, then straighten your body and reach to the sky. As you exhale, let out a big sigh of relief, bend at the waist, and drop your hands to the floor.

Next, use your hands to pat your entire body. Lightly pat every area of your body. This touching will energize you — it lets your body know that you know it's there.

When you feel energized, move your body around. Twist your body from side to side and shake out your arms and hands. Pick your feet up and put them down, and as you do this, make sounds — any expression of sound is helpful, even weird sounds. Then, shake everything out — your feet, legs, hands, and head. Continue to make sounds as you do this.

After moving around for five to ten minutes, pile several pillows into a mound and pound them with your fists or a plastic baseball bat. Be sure to express sound as you do this. Scream and make noise for all the times you didn't and wished you had. If you want, you can scream into the pillows.

Allow yourself five or ten minutes or more to do this; then, when you feel finished, let yourself rest. Find a comfortable place to sit or lie down. As you rest, notice how your body feels, and how you feel emotionally.

# Relationships

When we think about relationships, we think of an external process — our fulfillment will come from outside ourselves, from another person. The first step we often take to create a satisfying relationship is to look for someone else to satisfy our needs. But the key to successful relationships is actually within us, so it is no wonder that in looking outside ourselves for fulfillment, we often experience disappointment, resentment, and frustration.

Truly satisfying relationships begin inside us. Our primary relationship is our relationship with ourself. All other relationships are simply mirrors of it. Therefore, if we believe we are unlovable or if we are constantly critical of ourselves, we will continue to attract people and create situations that reinforce this belief. Conversely, as we learn to love ourselves, we will automatically receive the love and appreciation from others that we desire. If we are committed to ourselves and to the truth, we will attract others with equal commitment.

The following exercise may help you see how your beliefs about relationships directly affect the relationships you have, and it will give you an opportunity to create new beliefs that can fulfill you on the inside as well as the outside.

## EXERCISE 26

Think back to all the primary relationships you've had. In the space that follows, give a brief description of each of them. What were they like? How did you feel about them? What happened? Do you see any patterns repeating themselves? Examples follow on the next page.

**My Relationships**

1. *I went out with John, who seemed very interested in me but as soon as I became more interested in him, he seemed to withdraw. We broke up when I discovered he was seeing another woman.*

2. *I dated Steve, who pursued me for a long time until I agreed to go out. But he became more and more involved in his work and hardly had any time to see me. We broke up when he got a job out of state.*

1.

2.

3.

4.

5.

Once you identify a pattern or patterns, ask yourself how this reflects your internal relationship with yourself. For example, if I am attracted to critical people, this means I am being critical of myself, or if I am attracted to people who are emotionally supportive of me, this means I am supportive of myself. If people abandon me, it's an indication that I emotionally abandon myself. Sometimes the answers may not seem so evident. If so, ask the universe to reveal to you your part in the patterns, and be open to gaining more insight about your process. Caution: Often we are not aware of how much we control our relationships until we look at these patterns. Once you see what you've been doing, your tendency will be to blame yourself. Don't. The point is to see that you have the power to change the pattern of your relationships by working on your relationship with yourself, not to get hung up wishing you'd behaved differently in the past. You can always ask the universe for help in healing this pattern.

Write down your patterns and your solutions to them in the space provided on the next page.

| *My Patterns* | *Findings and Solutions* |
| --- | --- |
| 1. I find myself continually attracted to emotionally needy men (or women) like my father (or mother). | My partners mirror a needy part of me, a part that didn't get enough love and care when I was a child. I need to get in touch with that child in me and learn to take care of it. |
| 2. When I've been in a relationship for three to six months, I always want out. I want to start dating other people. I think there's something wrong with me. | I have a hard time standing up for myself and being honest in a relationship. I give up my individuality to the relationship and then I feel smothered and controlled. I can accept the way I am, instead of criticizing myself for this. I can begin to explore, through counseling, how I can assert myself in relationships rather than run away from them. |

|                  *My Patterns*                  |                  *Findings and Solutions*                  |

1.

2.

3.

4.

5.

## EXERCISE 27

Our past is often our most valuable teacher. In reviewing your life, are there times you wish you had followed your energy or trusted your instincts with someone or some situation, and you didn't? Write down these experiences.

**Examples:**

1. *I felt pressured to go out with Stan because he was someone my mother approved of. I wish I hadn't wasted my time.*
2. *I always wish I'd gone out with that guy in my theatre class in college, but I didn't because I felt too insecure.*
3. *I never talk to girls I really want to go out with. I'm afraid they won't like me.*

1.

2.

3.

4.




5.




Now take each of these memories, close your eyes, and visualize an image of yourself standing before you. Talk to yourself (out loud or internally). Tell yourself how you feel about each memory. If you blame yourself, express it. If you feel sad or frightened, express that. When you are done, tell the image of yourself what you learned from not doing what you might have.

Next, allow yourself to let go of each memory. You may want to say to yourself, "I understand and let go," or "I am now willing to release you," or "I am now willing to forgive you for this."

Is there anyone or any persons in your life *now* that you are attracted to in any way, but with whom you have been afraid to follow your energy? Write about this in the space below.

## EXERCISE 28

What would it be like to have a passionate love affair with yourself? What would it be like to follow your inner guidance — your energy — from moment to moment, to create and express beauty within and without? What would it be like to feel passionate about yourself and give yourself all the attention and care an impassioned lover would give you? Use the space below to describe it. Describe the richest, most vibrant life possible.

## EXERCISE 29

If there is a relationship in your life that you'd like to improve, write a description of how you'd like that relationship to be. Include important things like how you feel about each other, how you communicate, how you treat each other, what you enjoy doing together, and so on. Make it as real as possible.

Now ask yourself what part of you is afraid of having this, or is preventing you from creating this? Why? What is that part of you afraid of? Write your honest answers to these questions, as best you can. This is a process that will help you become aware of your own inner conflicts about relationships, and begin to clear them. Typically, we have a number of different types of realationships in our lives. Use the blank pages that follow for one or more types of relationship. For example, you might want to do the exercise with a romantic relationship in mind and then do the exercise with a work parental relationship in mind.

Note: Relationships are a complex, challenging, and fascinating area of our lives, from which we can learn a great deal. One of the best books to help us understand and learn from our relationships is *Embracing Each Other* by Drs. Hal and Sidra Stone, Nataraj/New World Library, 1989.

# Our Children

Deeply intimate relationships serve as our strongest mirrors; the people we are closest to will often express the feelings we have suppressed in ourselves. Children, in particular, can be mirrors of our feelings. Due to their uninhibited nature, they will often express or "act out" the feelings we have bottled up inside.

For example, if you try to appear calm and collected when inside you feel upset and angry, your children may reflect these feelings by becoming wild and disruptive. No matter how hard you may try to maintain control, they will tune into the chaotic energy inside you and reflect it in their behavior. Children are very sensitive to our true feelings. If you are not expressing your feelings, they will often do this for you.

Of course, most parents seek to protect their children from the problems and frustrations they themselves must face each day. They feel that sharing such feelings will only disturb children who may be too young to fully understand "adult" problems. But effective sharing does not mean dumping your anger on your children or involving them in the details of your concerns. You simply need to let your children know how you are truly feeling. For example, you might say, "I'm feeling really upset and frustrated because I've had a hard day. I'm mad at the world and at myself and at you. It's not your fault that I'm feeling this way. It would help, though, if you would go outside for a few minutes so I can have some peace and quiet to try to sort out my feelings." If you express your true feelings directly, your children will usually calm down. They feel comfortable with the truth, with the congruity between your feelings and your words.

The following exercises may guide you in discovering how your children mirror you. The exercises can encourage you to express your feelings more directly and honestly to your children.

## EXERCISE 30

In the first column, describe several "negative" interactions you've had with your child or children lately, or list some of your child's personality traits that bother you. Then, in the second column, ask yourself how these items mirror your own internal state. Once you have seen how their actions mirror your feelings, do not use this information to blame yourself or try to change or fix yourself. The gift is often in the seeing. Some examples follow.

| *Negative Interactions* | *How These Mirror You* |
| --- | --- |
| 1. *Sally is constantly rebelling.* | *I feel stuck with my responsibilities. Part of me wants to rebel against being such a "good girl," but I never let myself do that.* |
| 2. *Last Monday night, Billy was unhappy and critical of me and his brothers.* | *I've been very down on myself lately.* |
| 3. *My children have been clinging to me recently. They're so needy.* | *I feel like I never get time for myself. I never get my needs met. There's a child in me that needs to be loved, but I'm too busy being strong and competent.* |
| 4. *My children are self-centered and demanding. I feel like they run right over me.* | *I am the "martyr mother," always sacrificing for my kids. I need to honor that part of me that has demands, too, by learning to set boundaries with my kids and say "no" to them when appropriate.* |

|     | *Negative Interactions* | *How These Mirror You* |
| --- | --- | --- |
| 1.  |  |  |
| 2.  |  |  |
| 3.  |  |  |
| 4.  |  |  |
| 5.  |  |  |

| *Negative Interactions* | *How These Mirror You* |
| --- | --- |

6.

7.

8.

9.

10.

Next, list all the positive things you see in your children, and in the second column describe how these, too, mirror you. Examples are given.

| *Positive Interactions* | *How These Mirror You* |
|---|---|
| 1. My children decide they're going to do something and they do it. | I feel comfortable with my children's independence. I like to have time to do what I love to do. |
| 2. Rebecca seems to talk easily about how she feels. | I have been learning to accept my feelings. I express how I feel with my family. |
| 3. John enjoys playing the piano, and gave a recital in school. | I was never allowed to be truly creative as a child, but I am learning ways of expressing my creativity now. I am proud of my children's creativity. |

1.



2.



3.

|       *Positive Interactions*       |       *How These Mirror You*       |
| --- | --- |
| 4. | |
| 5. | |
| 6. | |
| 7. | |
| 8. | |
| 9. | |
| 10. | |

## EXERCISE 31

Practice telling the truth to your children and expressing your feelings honestly with them even if you feel vulnerable and uncomfortable about not being in control. Ask them how they feel about things and pay close attention to what they have to say. If you are tempted to give advice, ask them if they want to hear it first. If they don't, describe your feelings honestly instead.

Use the space below to record the results of these interactions with your children. Reviewing your notes from time to time will give you a sense of perspective on your evolving relationship with your children. It will also help you identify problem areas that recur.

## EXERCISE 32

Children have tremendous creativity, if it isn't stifled. They can help us to get back in touch with our own creativity if we let them. This exercise is intended to help you loosen up and have fun, and so be more creative, simply by playing with your children. If you don't have children, "borrow" a child to play with!

Sit down at a clean table with your child. Make sure there is plenty of space for each of you. Put crayons in lots of assorted colors (or you can use your own colored pens) in between you. Have plenty of unlined white paper for each of you. Now, without thinking too much, just start coloring. Pick your favorite colors and just let them move across the page. Don't worry about drawing anything in particular. When you feel you are finished, give the drawing to your child, and take theirs. Now, take a fresh sheet of paper and imitate as best as you can what the other drew.

For a variation on this exercise, have your child make a doodle on a piece of paper. Now, you finish the doodle by making something out of it. Then switch.

# Money

The creative energy of the universe is limitless and readily available to us at all times. Money is a symbol of our creative energy so, potentially, money is also readily available to us. The extent to which we are willing and able to express our creative energy effectively in the world determines how much money will be in our lives. A lack of money reflects the energy blockages within ourselves.

If you are not doing what you really love to do, if you don't believe you deserve to receive, or if your intuition nudges you to take action and you ignore it, your energy will be blocked; consequently, your money flow will be blocked as well. If you are doing what you love to do, and are willing to receive a return from your actions, the universe will reward you with an abundant flow of money in your life. As you learn to trust yourself and follow your inner guidance, you align yourself with the higher creative power that can provide for you on all levels, including the financial. To achieve financial balance and harmony in your life, you need to develop and integrate both the masculine principle of "doing" and expressing energy and the feminine principle of "being" and receiving energy.

Remember that true prosperity coming from an alignment of spirit and form does not involve excessive amounts of money to squander or waste. It involves an appropriate flow of money to do what you truly want in life and live a lifestyle that is in harmony with your being and with the earth.

## EXERCISE 33

This meditation may help free you of blocks to abundance you may have, and give you a vision of what prosperity is for you.

### *Meditation*

Start by breathing deeply for a few moments. Imagine that you're drawing a golden light into your body through your feet. As you inhale, the light moves upward through your feet, and continues to move upward through your entire body; as you exhale, it streams from the top of your head like a fountain, surrounding you with golden light.

Slowly inhale and feel this light filling all the cells of your body with abundance, opportunity, joy, creativity, and inner knowing. As you exhale, the light surrounds you with energy and power. Continue to draw the light in through you and surround yourself with it. As you do so, feel it dissolve any old ideas, negative beliefs, or blockages you have in your life. Visualize this light moving through you and healing you, transforming you into an open channel for prosperity. Spend a few moments with this image.

Next, imagine that this energy is now mirrored in your world. You now have abundance in your life. Take stock of your new status. What is your living environment like? What is your home like? What are you doing as a career? How are you expressing your creativity? What are your ideal relationships like? Thoroughly visualize how this prosperity has affected every aspect of your life.

If any negative thoughts surface, let them float by for now and stay gently focused on the prosperity that is yours, the wealth that is being mirrored in your life by the energy moving through your body. Visualize your prosperity exactly the way you would like it to be.

When you're ready, release this image, bring your awareness back into yourself, and feel yourself return to the room. Write a description of what you saw during this meditation and include a description of your ideal and prosperous life. You may want to pretend that you're writing about this to a friend.

**For example:** *Dear Susan: You should see my life. I am feeling great about myself and what has happened for me. My photography career has taken off. I am now doing portrait photography on a full-time basis. I am making enough money to do many of the things I've always wanted to do. I am taking a trip to Africa next spring . . . etc.*

## EXERCISE 34

*Meditation*

We can go within to seek answers to all we need to know. In this exercise, you will ask your inner guidance to show you what is blocking your energy — and therefore, financial prosperity — in your life.

Close your eyes and breathe deeply. Relax into a deep, quiet place inside, and ask to be in touch with your inner guidance. Ask yourself, "How am I blocking the flow of energy and wealth in my life now?" Be open to receive whatever answer might come to you, in words or an image. The answer may come right away or it may come in the next few hours, days, or weeks; don't be discouraged if you don't receive an answer right away.

The answer you seek can take any form. Your intuition might show you the face of someone you have unfinished business with, or perhaps your inner voice will give you a direct suggestion, such as, "Learn to say no more often," or "Take more risks." The guidance you receive may be something totally unexpected and may even seem unrelated to work or money. Whatever happens, trust what you hear; simply allow it to come forth.

When you have completed this first part of the exercise, make a list of the results. In the first column, list the ways that, according to your intuition, you are blocking yourself. In the second column, include any action you can take to unblock that energy so greater wealth can come to you now. Some examples follow.

| *How I Am Blocking Myself* | *What I Can Do About It* |
| --- | --- |
| 1. *I've been pushing myself because I'm afraid if I stop, no money will come in.* | *Take a day or two off and do things that are nourishing to myself, to open my ability to receive.* |
| 2. *I hold onto money tightly because I'm afraid I won't have enough.* | *Decide to give a small amount to a cause I support and see how I feel and what happens. Go out and buy something I want for myself now.* |

| *How I Am Blocking Myself* | *What I Can Do About It* |
| --- | --- |
| 1. | |
| 2. | |
| 3. | |
| 4. | |
| 5. | |

## EXERCISE 35

Draw a picture (or make a collage using pictures and words cut from magazines) of yourself living an abundant life on all levels — physical (material), emotional, mental, and spiritual. Include pictures or symbols of everything that's important to you on all these levels.

Use this page to continue your drawings or collage — and have fun!

# Work and Play

Our culture is obsessed with achievement and productivity. As a result we have an epidemic of workaholism in which most of us push ourselves much harder than is necessary or healthy. Some people carry the opposite polarity — they know how to relax and play, but have difficulty focusing and working hard enough to accomplish things.

When you're following your energy and doing what feels right to you, moment by moment, the distinction between work and play tends to dissolve. Work is no longer what you *have* to do and play what you *want* to do. When you are doing what you love, you may work harder and produce more than ever before, but it will often feel like play.

Finding our right work is an evolving process. At times, it may be appropriate to do work that we don't love in order to learn certain skills, or just to pay the bills while we are exploring, discovering, and growing in other ways. Also, our needs and desires change as we grow, so work that was suitable and enjoyable at one stage may be unfulfilling at another.

So, if you find yourself in a less than fully satisfying job, don't put yourself down or think you are doing something wrong. Just recognize that you are probably beginning to outgrow it, and start thinking, fantasizing, and investigating other possibilities.

The way to discover your right work at any stage of your life is to observe what you most love to do or feel interested in doing, and then take steps to do it. Your fantasies can tell you how you really want to be expressing yourself. Remember, the job you are seeking may not exist yet — it may be up to you to create it. The exercises that follow may help you discover your true work and dissolve the distinctions between work and play in your life.

## EXERCISE 36

Exploring your fantasies is a good first step toward finding work you love. Even very unrealistic fantasies, although they may not ever manifest in form, will help move you in the right direction for exploration and discovery.

In the first column, list the fantasies and dreams you entertain around work, career, and creativity. Then, visualize yourself doing what you've written down. For example, see yourself tap dancing on Broadway. Feel what it would be like for you to do what you love to do. Out of visualization often comes an inspiration for action.

In the second column, describe any actions you can take to explore your fantasies. Don't try to do all of these things at once or you will get overwhelmed. Choose one or two and try them. In a month or two, check the list again and see if you want to try another option. Let the next six months or year be a time of exploring and discovering the work that you would love to do. For example:

| Fantasies and Impulses | Action |
| --- | --- |
| 1. Tap dance on Broadway. | Call local dance studios and explore adult tap classes. Later, seek out a community theater group that may put together shows. Suggest a "dance show" and enlist to tap! |
| 2. Open my own ski shop. | Talk to the owner of the ski shop I go to and find out more about the business. |

| Fantasies and Impulses | Action |
|---|---|

1.

2.

3.

4.

5.

| *Fantasies and Impulses* | *Action* |
| --- | --- |
| 6. | |
| 7. | |
| 8. | |
| 9. | |
| 10. | |

## EXERCISE 37

Write down ten things you love to do, even if they don't seem to be work-related.

**Examples:**

1. *Organize things*
2. *Talk with people*
3. *Swim*
4. *Rearrange the furniture*
5. *Lift weights*

6. *Watch soap operas*
7. *Travel*
8. *Cook*
9. *Buy clothes for myself and others*
10. *Balance my checkbook*

1.

2.

3.

4.

5.

6.

7.

8.

9.

10.

Now, close your eyes, and imagine yourself doing some of these things and getting paid well for it. Take 5–10 minutes every day and repeat the visualization. If negative thoughts come up — for instance, if you find yourself saying that you couldn't possibly be paid for watching television — gently refocus your thoughts back to the positive. We sometimes close ourselves off to new opportunities by not believing they are possible. Suppose, for instance, that you have cooking and traveling on your list, and a week after you've been doing your visualization, you get an urge to call an old friend. You phone him — and he just happens to mention a job he's heard about for a cook on a cruise ship!

## EXERCISE 38

Affirmations can help you create what you want for yourself. Pick two of the affirmations below or make up some of your own and write them 10–20 times per day. Say them in front of a mirror in a firm voice. This can be very powerful. For example:

1. I, *(your name),* am now doing what I love to do and am richly rewarded for it.
2. I, _____, am now an open channel for creative ideas.
3. I, _____, now know exactly what I want to do to make plenty of money.
4. My work feels like play.
5. I, _____, trust the energy within me and am guided to my perfect job.

Use the space below to create your own affirmations. Continue on the next page if you want.

1.

2.

3.

4.

5.

# Health

The body is the barometer of our emotions. We may be able in our minds to deny what we are feeling, but our body always knows. If we let it, it can show us what is or is not working in our thinking, self-expression, and lifestyle. It can also tell us whether or not we have been trusting or ignoring our intuitive voice. When we trust ourselves, our bodies reflect this in increased health, aliveness, and beauty. When we don't trust ourselves and fail to follow our inner guidance, our aliveness decreases and our body reflects this in a loss of vitality, numbness, pain, and, eventually, physical disease.

Disease is a message sent by our bodies to tell us that we are not following our true energy or supporting our feelings. The body will continue to send signals until we get the message. These signals will start with relatively subtle feelings of tiredness and discomfort, and increase in urgency and intensity if we fail to pay attention and make the appropriate changes. We will receive increasingly stronger signals, including aches, pains, and minor illnesses; if we still don't change, a serious or even fatal illness or accident may eventually occur.

If you are suffering from physical discomfort or disease, *rest*. When you are quiet, ask your body what message your illness is conveying to you. Your body will always attempt to tell you what you need in order to heal yourself. The following exercises can help you learn to communicate more clearly with your body, and may help you uncover the cause of any disease you may be experiencing.

Obviously these exercises should be done in conjunction with appropriate medical attention, or other healing modalities, for specific problems.

## EXERCISE 39

*Meditation*

If a particular part of your body is sick or in pain, this meditation may help. Make yourself comfortable, take a few deep breaths, and completely relax your body and mind. Now direct your consciousness to the part of your body that needs healing, and ask that part what it is feeling and what it is trying to tell you. Be receptive to feeling and hearing what your body's message is. Ask that part of your body what you need to do to heal yourself. Pay attention and follow whatever it tells you.

If you have difficulty doing this process in meditation, try this written exercise: Get two colored pens. With your dominant hand, write a question to your body. With your other hand, and using the other colored pen, write spontaneously whatever comes to mind in answer to the question. At first it may be difficult to write with your nondominant hand, but do the best you can. Your dominant hand speaks for your conscious mind which is desiring information. Your nondominant hand speaks for your unconscious or intuitive mind, in this case representing the body's feelings.

**For example:**

Greg's dominant hand: *Back, why are you aching?*
Greg's nondominant hand (speaking for the back): *I'm carrying too much weight. I have too much responsibility. I need support.*
Greg's dominant hand: *What kind of support?*
Greg's nondominant hand: *I need Greg to have someone he can talk to about his feelings and problems. He tries to handle everything himself. Then I feel like I'm carrying the weight of the world on my shoulders.*

Continue this exercise until it feels complete for now.

## EXERCISE 40

*Meditation*

Poor health often can be the result of unexpressed emotion. If you are experiencing any disease in your life, this meditation may help you begin to uncover and express any feelings that may be underlying or even causing your illness.

Close your eyes and take a few deep breaths. As you relax, feel yourself let go of external concerns and gradually drop within yourself to your intuition. From this deep place within, allow an image of someone to come forward. This may be someone with whom you need to express some feelings, someone you've wanted to say something to for a long time, or someone with whom you have recently felt uncomfortable. It can be a "positive" or "negative" communication.

When this person is clearly before you, imagine you are saying whatever you have wanted to communicate to that person. Let out any and all unexpressed thoughts or feelings. Remember, any feelings you hold in are only hurting you. Unexpressed anger, which leads to resentment, is a major cause of disease in the body.

After you have expressed everything you need to say, tell this person, "I now release you (or I am now willing to release you) to your highest good," or, " I am willing to release you to the universe." Take a few deep breaths, and know that you have expressed and released everything you need to for right now.

Often, this process can make us aware of many things we have suppressed, so you may think you've said everything you need to say and then, a few hours later or a few days later, more feelings will surface and need to be expressed. If so, re-do the above exercise as often as you want, or do the following exercise.

## EXERCISE 41

You can also communicate any unexpressed feelings with a person by writing them a letter. On the next page or on a separate piece of paper, write a letter to someone you have needed to communicate with. Write everything you can think of that you've wanted to say. This is a time to express any thoughts you've had about the past, present, or future and a time to express all your feelings of blame, anger, hurt, sadness, love, etc. This is a safe place to express any feelings that have been buried within you and that may have been causing disease to your body. As you write you may get in touch with different emotions. For example, you may begin writing about anger and then begin expressing sadness, fear, and love. Trust your feelings and let them flow.

When you are finished, tear out this sheet and burn the letter. This will symbolize that you are emotionally letting go.

Again, if you find yourself feeling more feelings or having other thoughts that need to be expressed, re-do this exercise or go back t the previous meditation.

It may or may not be necessary to communicate any of these feelings to the person in question. Once you have done the meditation or written exercise one or more times, you may discover that you are gaining greater clarity about your feelings or are getting down to the essence of what's really bothering you. Just acknowledging these feelings to yourself may well be enough to heal them, especially if the person is no longer physically present in your life. If you feel the need to communicate with the person, however, write a real letter saying what you need to say as clearly and simply as possible, and then send it. Remember that if you can state the essence of your hurt or anger in a clear, direct way with as little blame or judgment as possible, you will have a better chance of being heard. Be sure to ask for what you want. Do this for your own clearing and healing, letting go of any particular expected response. If you have succeeded in expressing your deepest feelings, you will feel relieved and released. You may need to do this with more than one person — including parents, spouses, ex-lovers, friends, children. On the following page is an example of such a letter.

Susan,

I need to write this letter to express my feelings to you so that I don't carry them around inside of me anymore. I'm very hurt and angry that you have chosen to end our friendship without sharing with me your feelings or your reasons for doing so. I believe our friendship deserves better treatment than this. I'm hurt that you didn't trust me enough to tell me honestly what was going on for you. I have a lot of resentment about the way you handled this, which I'm trying to clear and release by writing to you, since it's very uncomfortable for me to have these kinds of feelings. I'd like you to write to me and tell me your feelings. It might help to clear things up.

Jane

## EXERCISE 42

To be truly full of health, we also need to learn to use our bodies physically in a way that is fun and joyful. Exercise too often implies work. We need to make our physical exercise more like play. Think of very young children, or animals. They don't need to go to the gym and work out to stay in shape. They move their bodies instinctively, stretching and running in ways that are simple and playful. This exercise will help you put joy in your movements.

Find an area in your home with a good deal of open space. Move furniture around if you need to — just enough so that you have a clear area for about one body-length in each direction. Put on some music that represents your current mood, or a mood you would like to be in right now. Are you feeling excited, tired, somewhat edgy, or overextended? Stand in the middle of the space you have just created and start to move your head to the music. Without any strain or effort, slowly let your head move and change, remembering to let your jaw hang loose. As the music plays, let your body start to move with it, slowly letting each part of the body join in, similar to the tuning up of an orchestra. Let the shoulders join in when they're ready, let the hands find their expression. Slowly, work your way down your body until all the parts of you are "playing in the orchestra." When you've reached your feet, start to move back up the body and include all the parts of your body that want to move, always remembering the rhythm of the music. Continue playing music and moving to it as long as it feels good.

When you feel finished, sit or lie down for a few minutes and reflect on how your body feels. Where do you feel some loosening of your muscles? Where do you feel you need to stretch? Complete this exercise by noting these body parts and either stretch them right now or remember them for tomorrow or the next time you repeat this exercise. Notice how you feel emotionally. This is an excellent time to spend a few minutes meditating, saying affirmations, or just relaxing.

## EXERCISE 43

In the space that follows, describe what perfect health for you would be like. How would you look, feel, and act? Include spiritual, mental, emotional as well as physical aspects of health. Now, visualize what you describe, and affirm that this state of perfect health is a reality in your life right now.

# Your Perfect Body

Your perfect body is the one you already have. It's the body your spirit has created as your expression in physical form. To get a sense of how beautiful our bodies really are, watch a group of young children playing naturally together. Though they may be quite different in size, coloring, and shape, they are each beautiful in their own way. Watch animals in a natural setting and see how beautiful they are. Young children and animals are so beautiful because they are filled with life force and move freely with that energy. Unfortunately, as we grow up, we are conditioned not to trust and follow our life energy. Our bodies pay the price. Also, most civilized human beings have not learned to love, appreciate, or care for our bodies, and our bodies begin to show this lack of love and care. To allow your body to express its true beauty, you must develop a loving, supportive relationship with it. This can take time and patience.

The health and well-being of our bodies is strongly connected to our emotional well-being. We are much more likely to be physically healthy, vital, and attractive if and when we are feeling emotionally secure and fulfilled. Our emotional wounds, conflicts, and blocks are often expressed physically in our bodies. Our feelings about our bodies are connected to our core feelings about our identity and self-worth. Therefore, our body issues are deep and complex. There are no simple solutions, but if we are willing to do the inner work of emotional and spiritual healing, as well as physical healing, our problems with our bodies can lead us to wholeness on all levels.

One of the most common ways that our emotional difficulties manifest physically is in our relationship to food, through weight problems (overweight or underweight) and eating disorders. Our relationship with food has deep emotional roots, connected with our childhood feelings toward our families, and with issues of scarcity, nurturing, self-love, personal boundaries, and intimacy.

We are an addictive society, and a great many people these days have an addictive relationship to food. That is, we use food compulsively to control or suppress emotions, to fill emotional needs, to avoid confronting other issues, and so on.

If you have food addictions or an eating disorder, the exercises in this chapter, while possibly providing some valuable insight, will not be sufficient to help you deal with the problem. They may not even be appropriate for you, at least until you do the primary work of confronting and healing the addictive behavior with professional or group support.

If you do have addictive patterns with food or any eating disorder such as serious overeating, anorexia, or bulimia, I urge you to seek professional counseling. There are many wonderful therapists and programs specializing in these problems. And there is Overeaters Anonymous, a twelve-step program with free meetings in most cities.

If you do not have food addictions or serious body issues, or you have already done effective work on them, you may find that the exercises in this chapter can help you restore a natural, trusting relationship with your body.

Having a beautiful body starts with following the natural flow of your energy. This means trying to sleep, eat, rest, and move when *you* want. It means learning to trust yourself.

The main obstacle to trusting ourselves is that most of us have not yet learned how. As children, we unquestioningly adopt parental and societal rules, habits, and thoughts about how we treat our bodies. These include eating at times convenient to others, not ourselves, and finishing our plates in order to receive a reward. Even as adults, although we may have radically changed our childhood habits, our lifestyles are still based on our reactions to external pressures and attitudes. Grown-up though we may be, we have yet to establish a direct connection to our true, spontaneous nature — our essential self. Because of this, it is difficult to understand and respond to the natural needs of our bodies.

In learning to trust yourself, you must first risk acting on what your body is telling you. In the beginning, you may receive information only from your head, rather than your intuition, but the more you risk acting on what you hear inside yourself, the more you will open your inner channel and the clearer your intuitive messages will become.

Your body knows what's good for it, and you need to be open to whatever it might request of you, whether it is to stay in bed or to get up early and work hard the whole day long. At first, you may find yourself doing the opposite of everything you have been doing. For example, if you've been working constantly, you may want to spend a few days (or months!) resting, relaxing, and playing, doing what you've been denying yourself. Or, if you tend toward lethargy, you may need to get your body moving. Let yourself experiment as much as possible. Eventually, you will find a balance, and this time it will stem from that deep source of balance within.

The following exercises can help identify negative beliefs or old attitudes you've had about your body, and pave the way for a more deeply intuitive understanding of what you truly need.

## EXERCISE 44

Sit down and reflect on all the old ideas and beliefs you have about your body, food, and exercise. Try to go back and recall everything anyone ever told you about food. These may be statements you heard from your mother or father, or beliefs acquired from television or magazines. Let them all come to the surface. Write down as many as you can think of. Next to each one, write an affirmation that will balance these beliefs. Examples follow.

| *Negative Beliefs* | *Affirmations* |
| --- | --- |
| *1. I don't like my body.* | *I love and appreciate my body.* |
| *2. I'm too fat (or too thin).* | *My body is beautiful.* |
| *3. I gain weight every time I look at food.* | *I can safely enjoy looking at and eating food because my body is slender and healthy.* |
| *4. I'll never have the kind of body I want.* | *I, (your name), now have the body I want.* |

| _Negative Beliefs_ | _Affirmations_ |
|---|---|

1.

2.

3.

4.

5.

| *Negative Beliefs* | *Affirmations* |
| --- | --- |
| 6. | |
| 7. | |
| 8. | |
| 9. | |
| 10. | |

## EXERCISE 45

Using any old ideas and beliefs you have had about your body, describe how you have been controlling yourself rather than following your natural rhythm. Next to each statement, list ways you are willing to let go of this control and allow your natural rhythm to come through.

If you are accustomed to controlling yourself, letting go can be an uncomfortable experience. Initially, you may want to practice doing this in one area of your life only. Move on to the next area only when you are comfortable with this process. Some examples follow.

| *How I Control* | *Ways to Let Go* |
|---|---|
| 1. *I push myself to keep going when I'm really tired.* | *For one week, I can rest when my body wants to rest, instead of pushing myself.* |
| 2. *I am constantly on a "controlled" diet where I deprive myself of almost everything I really like.* | *For one week, instead of dieting, I'll let myself eat what I really want.* |
| 3. *I insist that I run five miles a day whether I feel like it or not.* | *This week, I will let myself run only when I want, and then only as far as I want.* |

1.


2.

|     | *How I Control* | *Ways to Let Go* |
| --- | --- | --- |
| 3.  |     |     |
| 4.  |     |     |
| 5.  |     |     |
| 6.  |     |     |
| 7.  |     |     |
| 8.  |     |     |
| 9.  |     |     |
| 10. |     |     |

## EXERCISE 46

Learning to appreciate and love yourself is an important part of developing your perfect body. All things grow more beautiful when they are nourished by love and appreciation.

In the space below, write down as many things as you can think of that you can do to appreciate yourself. Be sure to focus on things you can do for your body.

**Examples:**

*1. Take a hot bath.*

*2. Buy fresh flowers for myself.*

*3. Eat a delicious gourmet meal of natural, healthful foods.*

*4. Splurge on a professional massage.*

*5. Go swimming.*

*6. Take a half day just to pamper myself — eat a wonderful meal, listen to classical music, and lie around relaxing.*

*7. Take a long, solitary walk and enjoy the pleasure of my own company.*

*8. Join a health club and go twice a week.*

1.

2.

3.

4.

5.

6.

7.

8.

9.

10.

## EXERCISE 47

If you always wait (weight) to be, do, or have what you want, your energy may become blocked and your body may reflect this in excess weight. By expressing yourself directly and doing what you want, when you want, energy will move freely through your body.

What have you been "weighting" for — what have you been "weighting" to say, do, or be? In one column, write down anything you have been "weighting" to do.

Is there anything you'd like to change about this? In the second column, list what you would like to do to put a stop to your "weighting." If you do not want to take action on some of the issues you've been "weighting" to handle, you may want to put a date by your plans to solidify your action. Examples follow.

| *What I Am "Weighting" For* | *Action I Will Take* |
|---|---|
| 1. I've been wanting to do more dancing and always say I'll have more time later, but I never make room for it. | I'm going to take one dance class a week starting this week. |
| 2. I keep wanting to call my ex-husband and confront him with the fact that he still owes me $10,000. | Take an assertiveness class, then call or write him. |
| 3. I keep "weighting" to look beautiful until I have lost weight. | I can buy a dress that makes me look beautiful right now at my current weight. I can make an effort to look pretty now. |
| 4. I keep "weighting" for the right time to ask my boss for a raise. | First I'll talk over with a friend my fears about this. Then, I'll ask my boss for a raise by the end of the month. |

| *What I Am "Weighting" For* | *Action I Will Take* |
| --- | --- |
| 1. | |
| 2. | |
| 3. | |
| 4. | |
| 5. | |

| *What I Am "Weighting" For* | *Action I Will Take* |
| --- | --- |

6.


7.


8.


9.


10.

## EXERCISE 48

Many people use food to change their natural energy level. Those with too much nervous energy may use it to slow themselves down, and people who feel a need for a pick-up may eat sugar or drink coffee or other stimulants to try to "get going." This use of food, however, interferes with and distorts the body's natural rhythm and flow of energy.

What would happen if you were not controlling your energy with food? If you didn't have to stop yourself from being who you are, what would your energy be like?

Take a moment to relax, then close your eyes and drop into that deepest place inside yourself. Ask your intuition to reveal an image of your true energy — what you would be like if you were not using anything to pace or change yourself.

Describe this in the space below and on the following page.

# Life and Death

To be alive means to choose to follow the flow of energy within ourselves. Whenever we trust in, and live according to, the flow of our life energy, our channel expands and fills our physical body with energy. Even our cells are renewed and nourished, so we feel vital and healthy. The more the life force flows through us, the more alive we feel.

Death results when we choose, either consciously or unconsciously, to close down our channel, to block the flow of life energy in our being. When we turn away from following our own inner truth, our body suffers from the decreased life force that results. Gradually we deteriorate, physically, emotionally, and mentally. We all have seen how stress and emotional blockages have taken their toll on us and those around us — a haggard expression, the deep lines of worry etched in the face, constant back pain, and eventually, serious — even terminal — illness.

The following exercises can help you to become more aware of the direction you are choosing — toward life or toward death — in every aspect of your life. They may help you to make the choice each day to live fully and deeply in the light of renewed vigor and joy.

## EXERCISE 49

In the space below, write an ideal scene of how your life would be if you were able to really love and trust yourself and live fully from your own inner sense of truth and integrity. What would it be like to make daily choices that allow you to feel fully alive?

Now, think about and write down the habits, concerns, or fears that keep you from being able to live fully and freely.

## EXERCISE 50

In the space below, list the commitment(s) you are willing to make at this moment to choose life. **For example:**

1. *I am now willing to work four days a week instead of five. I will work less and relax more. This will renew and nourish me.*
2. *I will stop stuffing my feelings. I will find a good therapist who can help me express my feelings.*
3. *I will spend one evening a week working on my creative project.*
4. *One day a month, I will commit to following my intuition every moment of that day. I will keep a special journal during that time to record the results of this decision.*

1.


2.


3.


4.


5.

# Transforming the World

Transformation begins on an individual level and moves out into the world. The more I'm learning to trust my intuition and act on it, and the more I'm willing to experience and accept all my feelings, the more the energy of the universe can move through me. As it comes through, it heals and transforms me and everyone and everything around me.

This is true for each one of us. The more you are willing to trust and be yourself, the more life energy will move through you. Everyone around you will benefit from your energy and begin to trust and be more themselves. In turn, they become powerful channels for everyone in their sphere of influence. And so, transformation spreads rapidly throughout the world.

You may have heard of the "hundredth-monkey syndrome." In Japan, in 1952, scientists were studying the behavior of wild monkeys. The principle food of these monkeys was sweet potatoes. One day, they noticed one monkey do something they had never seen before — she washed her potato before she ate it. She repeated this behavior on subsequent days, and soon they noticed several other monkeys washing their potatoes before eating them. More and more monkeys began to do this. Then, in 1958, after all monkeys on the island were exhibiting this new behavior, scientists on nearby islands began to report that monkeys on their islands were also beginning to wash their potatoes. There was no physical connection between the islands, and no one had transported any monkeys from one island to another.

This study illustrates something of overwhelmingly powerful importance for the human race and for our planet. Washing potatoes was a new level of evolution for these monkeys, and when enough of them had accepted it, it was apparently transferred to the monkeys on surrounding islands without any physical contact or direct communication.

This is how the evolution of consciousness takes place. Every individual's consciousness is connected to, and is a part of, the mass consciousness. When a small but significant number of individuals have moved into a new level of awareness and significantly changed their behavior, that change is felt in the entire mass consciousness. Every other individual is then moved in the direction of that change. And the whole thing may have started with one individual who first made the leap.

As we make the transition from the old world to the new, things may appear to be going from bad to worse. It may seem as if many things that used to work are not working anymore. Actually, things are falling apart and will continue to do so with even greater intensity, but this is a positive, natural part of the process of change. The transition can be exciting if we can open our eyes to the profound changes that are occurring, and welcome them.

We are now learning how to live in accordance with the true laws of the universe. When we live in harmony with the universe, we have totally rich lives, full of vitality, joy, power, love, and abundance on every level. Although letting go of the old world may be difficult at times, it is well worth whatever it takes to make the transition into the new world. This is a process that cannot be pushed or hurried. We are challenged to appreciate and take with us the valuable aspects of our old way of being while moving, at our own pace, forward into the new. It is a lifelong journey.

The following exercises may help you in making your journey from the old world to the new world with joy and awareness.

## EXERCISE 51

*Meditation*

Close your eyes and take a few deep breaths. Let go of any outside concerns and drop into a quiet place within yourself. Imagine that you are under the stars in a peaceful place. A huge bonfire rages in front of you. Feel the warmth of the fire and the peacefulness of the air around you. Then, slowly begin to move around the fire, and as you do, throw into the fire anything that represents the old way of life for you. Move around the fire saying, "I now release struggle in my life. I now release fear, sickness, or disharmony in my world. I now release and toss into the fire any and all poverty. I now release _____

_____

_____." (Fill in the blank with as many items as you want.)Keep moving around the fire, letting go of anything that is an old way for you, feeling yourself lighten up as you do.

When you feel you've released whatever you no longer need from your old way of life, walk away from the fire and stand under the stars. Rejoice in the lightness of unburdening yourself.

Imagine yourself opening your arms wide and welcoming in the new. You've created a void by releasing the old, so now you can fill that void with the new. Stay open to images of what this newness is. As you receive images of the new, you may want to say, "I now receive ease and joy in my life. I now receive abundance. I now claim a peaceful world. I now receive

_____

_____." (Again, fill in the blank.) Stand there as long as you want, as long as you feel willing to receive and claim the gifts of the universe. When you feel ready, leave the stars and the bonfire and feel yourself come back into the room refreshed and filled with the energy of your new world.

On the next two pages, list the things you are now willing to release. Then, tear out these pages and burn them to symbolize your release of the old.

In the page provided, list the new things you are now ready to receive. Claim these as yours.

........................................................................

*Things I Am Willing to Release*

*Things I Am Willing to Release*

*New Things I Am Now Ready to Receive*

## EXERCISE 52

In the space provided describe your new way of life. Write it in the present tense as if it were already true. What does it look and feel like for you and for the world around you? Spend a few minutes every day visualizing this. As you give the vision more attention, notice how it will gradually start to manifest as a reality in your life.

# Making Change

How can we take action to make positive change in the world? When faced with this challenge, many of us respond in one of the following ways:

1. We become overwhelmed, feeling that nothing we can do will be of any use, and thus we do nothing.

2. Driven by conscious or unconscious fear and despair, we adopt a cause or a course of action. Then we struggle, fight, or sacrifice to try to "save the world." This way of going about things tends to perpetuate the very problems we're trying to solve.

There is another alternative. True transformation, on a personal and planetary level, is achieved as more and more of us listen to our own inner guidance and follow our own life flow, thereby fulfilling our life purpose and contributing to the world through our greatest gifts. As we do what we love, we experience pleasure, excitement, and aliveness, and the world is enhanced by our very presence. From this energy, any type of direct social or political action we take is tremendously effective.

These exercises can help you find ways to make effective positive change in the world.

## EXERCISE 53

*Meditation*

Get in a comfortable position, relax and close your eyes. Breathe slowly and deeply, and as you release each breath, move into a deeper level of relaxation. Bring your awareness into a deep place within, the place where you are connected with your own greatest wisdom. Ask your inner guidance to let you know what your role is in helping to bring positive change into the world. Then, sit quietly and be receptive to what comes to you in feelings, words, or images. If you wish, ask for clarification or more specifics. If nothing seems to come, let it go, and know that it will come to you in some form at some time in the near future. Repeat this meditation whenever you wish, and more awareness and information may unfold.

Some examples of awareness that might come through this meditation are:

*"I have a natural gift for teaching. I help people learn how to live more fulfilling lives."*

*"I'm great at organizing and taking care of business. I need to seek a worthy cause that needs my talents, and help them be more successful at what they're trying to do."*

*"My primary gift is nurturing my children, my friends, myself. As I nurture others I heal and empower them, and when I nurture myself, I set a good example for others."*

*"I have a lot of good ideas about how I'd like to see things done in the city. I'd like to run for city council."*

*"I'm here to lighten things up. I love to have fun and make people laugh. I just need to keep doing the things that are fun for me, and including other people in my fun."*

## EXERCISE 54

Write a list of things you enjoy doing that contribute something to the world and/or that could help make positive change in some way, small or large. Include things even if they only affect one or a few other people, or animals, or a small part of the earth.

Every day (or once a week) pick one thing and do it, with full conscious knowledge that you are doing something to bring positive change into this world.

1.

2.

3.

4.

5.

6.

7.

8.

9.

10.

# Recommended Resources

## BOOKS

Gawain, Shakti. *Living in the Light,* Revised Edition. Nataraj/New World Library, 1998.

Gawain, Shakti. *Creating True Prosperity Workbook.* Nataraj/New World Library, 1998.

Gawain, Shakti. *The Four Levels of Healing: A Guide to Balancing the Spiritual, Mental, Emotional, and Physical Aspects of Life.* Nataraj/New World Library, 1997.

Gawain, Shakti. *Creating True Prosperity.* Nataraj/New World Library, 1997.

Gawain, Shakti. *Creative Visualization,* Revised Edition. Nataraj/New World Library, 1995.

Gawain, Shakti. *The Path of Transformation: How Healing Ourselves Can Change the World.* Nataraj/New World Library, 1993.

Gawain, Shakti. *Return to the Garden.* Nataraj/New World Library, 1989.

Nelson, Martia. *Coming Home: The Return to True Self.* Nataraj/New World Library, 1993.

Roberts, Jane. *The Nature of Personal Reality.* Amber-Allen Publishing/New World Library, 1994.

Stone, Sidra. *The Shadow King.* Nataraj/New World Library, 1997.

Stone, Hal and Sidra. *Embracing Our Selves: The Voice Dialogue Manual.* Nataraj/New World Library, 1993.

Stone, Hal and Sidra. *Embracing Each Other: Relationship as Teacher, Healer, and Guide.* Nataraj/New World Library, 1993.

## AUDIO TAPES

Gawain, Shakti. *Living in the Light: Book on Tape.* Revised and abridged. Nataraj/New World Library, 1998.

Gawain, Shakti. *The Four Levels of Healing: A Guide to Balancing the Spiritual, Mental, Emotional, and Physical Aspects of Life.* Nataraj/New World Library, 1997.

Gawain, Shakti. *Creating True Prosperity: Book on Tape.* Nataraj/New World Library, 1997.

Gawain, Shakti. *Creative Visualization Meditations.* Nataraj/New World Library, 1996.

Gawain, Shakti. *Creative Visualization: Book on Tape.* Revised. Nataraj/New World Library, 1995.

Gawain, Shakti. *The Path of Transformation: Book on Tape.* Abridged version. Nataraj/New World Library, 1993.

Stone, Hal and Sidra. *Meeting Your Selves.* Delos, 1990.

Stone, Hal and Sidra. *The Child Within.* Delos, 1990.

Stone, Hal and Sidra. *Meet Your Inner Critic.* Delos, 1990.

Stone, Hal and Sidra. *Meet the Pusher.* Delos, 1990.

Stone, Hal and Sidra. *The Dance of Selves in Relationship.* Delos, 1990.

Stone, Hal and Sidra. *Understanding Your Relationships.* Delos, 1990.

Stone, Hal and Sidra. *Affairs and Attractions.* Delos, 1990.

Stone, Hal and Sidra. *Decoding Your Dreams.* Delos, 1990.

(All of Hal and Sidra Stone's tapes are available through Delos. See address on the next page.)

## WORKSHOPS

Shakti Gawain gives talks and leads workshops all over the United States and in many other countries. She also conducts retreats, intensives, and training programs. If you would like to be on her mailing list and receive workshop information, contact:

Shakti Gawain, Inc.
P.O. Box 377, Mill Valley, CA 94942
Telephone: (415) 388-7140
Fax: (415) 388-7196
e-mail: sg@nataraj.com
www.shaktigawain.com

Shakti and her husband, Jim Burns, rent rooms and a guest cottage at their beautiful estate on the Hawaiian island of Kaua'i. For information or to make a reservation, contact:

Kai Mana
P.O. Box 612, Kilauea, HI 96754
Telephone: (808) 828-1280 or (800) 837-1782
Fax: (808) 828-6670

For information about Drs. Hal and Sidra Stone's workshops and trainings, contact:

Delos
P.O. Box 604, Albion, CA 95410
Telephone: (707) 937-2424
e-mail: delos@mcn.org

Nataraj* Publishing, a division of New World Library,
is dedicated to publishing books and tapes
that inspire and challenge us to improve the
quality of our lives and our world.

Our books and tapes are available
in bookstores everywhere.
For a catalog of our complete library
of fine books and cassettes contact:

Nataraj Publishing/New World Library
14 Pamaron Way
Novato, CA 94949
Tel: (415) 884-2100
Fax: (415) 884-2199
Or call toll-free: (800) 972-6657
Catalog requests: Ext. 50
Ordering: Ext. 52
E-mail: escort@nwlib.com
http://www.nwlib.com

*Nataraj* is a Sanskrit word referring to the creative, transformative power of the universe.